T0347263

Irish Political Studies Data Yearbook 2002

EDITORS

Karin Gilland • Fiachra Kennedy

A Supplement to *Irish Political Studies* Vol.17

FRANK CASS
LONDON • PORTLAND, OR

First Published in 2003 in Great Britain by
FRANK CASS PUBLISHERS
Crown House, 47 Chase Side, Southgate
London, N14 5BP

and in the United States of America by
FRANK CASS PUBLISHERS
c/o ISBS, 920 NE 58th Avenue, Suite 300
Portland, Oregon, 97213-3786

Website: www.frankcass.com

British Library Cataloguing in Publication Data

Irish political studies data yearbook 2002
1. Ireland – Politics and government – 1949– – Periodicals
2. Northern Ireland – Politics and government – 1994– –
Periodicals
I. Gilland, Karin II. Kennedy, Fiachra
320.9′415′05

ISBN 0-7146-5519-8 (cloth)
ISBN 0-7146-8411-2 (paper)
ISSN 0790-7184

This volume is published as a supplement to *Irish Political Studies* Vol.17

Printed in Great Britain by Antony Rowe Ltd, Chippenham, Wiltshire

CONTENTS

Reports

Data Section

ingenta

From Volume 17, Number 1, 2002, this journal is available to institutional subscribers online at *www.ingenta.com*

For details of past and future contents of this and our other journals as well as guidance on gaining access to this journal online, please visit our website at *www.frankcass.com/jnls*

WHAT IS THE IRISH SOCIAL SCIENCE DATA ARCHIVE?

James P. McBride

Director, Irish Social Science Data Archive

The Irish Social Science Data Archive (ISSDA) was established in 2000, as a joint initiative of University College Dublin and the Economic and Social Research Institute. Based in UCD, the archive is a component of the Institute for the Study of Social Change. Its establishment and development has been facilitated by grants from the HEA's Programme for Research in Third Level Institutes, part of the National Development Plan.

Datasets

ISSDA has been established to improve access for researchers and students to social science datasets, both Irish and international. The Archive operates with the support and co-operation of the Central Statistics Office (CSO), and is now the CSO's preferred first point of contact for those seeking its data for academic research purposes. A full listing of the Archive's catalogue is available on the ISSDA website, at <http://www.ucd.ie/~issda/data.htm>. This includes:

- CSO datasets, such as the Quarterly National Household Survey (QHNS), Household Budget Survey (HBS), and a five per cent anonymised individual level sample of the 1996 Census of Population;
- ESRI datasets, such as the complete span of the School Leavers Survey, from 1980–99, and the Irish data from the European Community Household Panel (ECHP) survey;
- international social science datasets, such as the Eurobarometer (since 1990), the ISSP (currently from 1985–98), and the European Values Survey for 1981 and 1990;
- ISSDA is the nominated repository for data resulting from the Irish National Election Study, and will make these data widely available in due course.

ISSDA will endeavour to, over time, enhance its current collection and expand into other social science data areas.

Connectivity

ISSDA is a part of the international community of data archives, through its membership of the Council of European Social Science Data Archives (CESSDA) and the International Association of Social Science Information and Technology (IASSIST). CESSDA (<http://www.nsd.uib.no/cessda/>) membership plugs the Irish social science community into an additional resource. The CESSDA network allows for a limited amount of data sharing among its constituent member countries. If a researcher comes across a dataset in the archive of, for instance, the UK Data Archive, which is not available in the ISSDA catalogue, it may be possible to acquire it via the CESSDA network. Contact ISSDA for further details.

Access to ISSDA Data

Data can be acquired from ISSDA either via the Internet (excluding ECHP or CSO datasets) or on CD-ROM. Before access is granted, the relevant data request form must be completed and returned to ISSDA. These are available from the Data section of the ISSDA website (<http://www.ucd.ie/~issda>). Access to ISSDA datasets for non-funded research use is free, subject to minor carriage and media costs, if data are required on CD-ROM.

ISSDA Newsletter

ISSDA produces an occasional newsletter with information on the archive's holdings and activities. This is available either by e-mail (plain text version), or from the ISSDA website (in Portable Document Format [PDF]) The current edition is available at <http://www.ucd.ie/~issda/documentation/issue02.pdf>. If you would like to receive the e-mail version of the newsletter, which is usually available at least a week before the PDF version, please email <issda@ucd.ie>.

Future Developments

As ISSDA develops and grows, it is hoped that it will be able to develop its activities in the following areas:

- The creation of an ISSDA User Group. This could take a number of forms, for instance as a LISTSERV mailing list, to encourage discussion of the archive and its services among a wider group than is currently the case.

- Development of teaching packages. Using the sizeable (and growing) ISSDA collection, it is the intention of ISSDA to develop resources to assist in the acquisition of basic data analysis skills.
- Acquisition of 'old' data. In addition to the contemporary datasets held by ISSDA, it is hoped to expand the archives holding by acquiring older datasets, for instance by exploiting data held by the ESRI and CSO stretching back to the 1970s.

If you have any comments or queries regarding ISSDA, please e-mail me at <issda@ucd.ie>. Full information and contact details for the archive are available at the website: <http://www.ucd.ie/~issda>.

PUBLIC OPINION IN THE REPUBLIC OF IRELAND – 2001

Pat Lyons

Public Opinion & Political Behaviour Research Programme
Institute for the Study of Social Change
University College Dublin*

Introduction

In 2001, eight opinion polls were published in national newspapers (Independent Newspapers Ltd and *The Irish Times*).[1] Three were under-taken by MRBI for *The Irish Times*. All of the MRBI polls were undertaken in the first six months of the year. The remaining five surveys were taken by IMS for Independent Newspapers. The taking of opinion polls was strongly influenced in the first half of 2001 by the 'foot and mouth' crisis. Only one IMS poll was undertaken during the crisis on 8 March, in urban areas. The results of this survey tend to attenuate responses that are known to have a rural basis, e.g. support for Fine Gael. The results for the last IMS survey of the year were weighted, which is a little unusual. There seem to have been problems with the sample drawn with an under-representation of some sub groups (25–34 years, 65 + years, farmers, people living in Connaught/ Ulster and urban areas) and over-representation of others (35–49 years and those living in rural areas). In this report, a brief examin-ation will be made of the state of affairs in 2001 with regard to politics and the economy. Then there will be an overview of the key issues that attracted opinion poll questions and, finally, there will be a look at how opinions were shaping up with the countdown to the 2002 general election.

Satisfaction with Politics and the Economy

Party, Leader and Government Support

MRBI adopted a new adjustment or weighting procedure in estimating party support (vote intention if there was an election) from November 1999. This adjustment exists because of the increasingly salient effects of declining voter turnout in elections and its impact on intention-to-vote questions asked in surveys. MRBI, on the basis of research undertaken after the 1997 general election, justified the adoption of this new methodology on the basis that support in its polls for Fianna Fáil is inflated by voters who never actually turn out to vote. Such misreporting by voters results in an overestimation of support for Fianna Fáil by about six per cent compared to the actual election result (Jones, 2001: 164–5).

Compared to MRBI estimates, support for Fianna Fáil as measured by IMS was consistently higher throughout 2001. If anything, the difference in estimates appeared to grow. For example the difference in the first polls in 2001 was five per cent. By December this gap had grown to 13 per cent. Over 2001 both IMS and MRBI polls found that support for Fianna Fáil support increased. Support for Fine Gael and Labour remained more of less constant. The smaller parties tended to follow a similar pattern of little real change in support – quite often below five per cent, which is problematic for interpretation given that the sampling error for national polls is plus or minus three per cent.

Looking at IMS polls, satisfaction with the performance of Bertie Ahern remained reasonably constant throughout 2001 at 68 per cent. This absolute level of support given the duration of the government was also impressive. The Tanaiste, Mary Harney, also sustained a high satisfaction rating throughout 2001 of 59 per cent. Within Fine Gael there was a change of leadership in February when Michael Noonan took over from John Bruton, who had been leader since November 1990. Satisfaction with the leader of Fine Gael slipped significantly from 44 per cent to 32 per cent in the IMS polls. In general, satisfaction with the Fine Gael leadership followed a downward trend throughout the life of the twenty-eighth Dáil. The emergence of Noonan as leader only provided a brief respite to this trend.[2] Satisfaction with the Labour Party leader also declined dramatically in 2001 by 13 points in the IMS polls. Unlike the case of Fine Gael supporters (who moved from being satisfied to 'don't know') this decline was also marked by a jump in dissatisfaction of 14 points. In general, the popularity of opposition party leaders declined dramatically in 2001, while those in power retained a high level of support.

Satisfaction with the Fianna Fáil/Progressive Democrat minority coalition government grew continuously from September 2000 to the end of 2001. Within the year September 2000 to September 2001 satisfaction with the government increased an unprecedented 21 points from 43 per cent to 64 per cent.[3] However, within the 2001 calendar year, government satisfaction stayed largely constant at the 60 per cent mark for both IMS and MRBI. Such results indicate the need for some caution in interpreting and presenting data of this type – the timescale used can be crucial in 'showing' trends over time.

Economy

The budget announced in December 2000, while popular among the Irish public, proved to be rather unpopular with the European Commission, who felt that the stability pact criteria on inflation would be infringed. In fact, during 2001 the inflation rate in Ireland moved steadily upwards. In a post-budget MRBI poll, a slim majority of the public (51 per cent) felt that their standard of living would remain the same while slightly over a third (35 per cent) felt it would increase.[4] Seven out of ten respondents thought the budget was good for the country. When those interviewed were posed the hypothetical option of foregoing promised tax cuts in the budget of December 2001 in order to improve the health service, three out of four (74 per cent) agreed to this option.[5] A subsequent MRBI poll in May showed that Irish public was evenly split over whether or not economic growth would continue.[6]

In December, IMS followed up on this theme, by stating explicitly that there was an economic slowdown in Ireland, and asked respondents how long they thought this downturn would last. Notwithstanding the complexity (and bias) of such a question, half felt it would last one to two years.[7] By the end of 2001 a small majority (51 per cent) felt that their standard of living had remained the same, with a third thinking it got better.[8] It is interesting to see that the same frequencies for budget satisfaction at the start of the year prevailed for assessment of change in the standard of living at the end of the year.

According to some commentators one of the pillars behind Ireland's economic growth since 1987 has been 'social partnership'. Having lived with social partnership for fourteen years the Irish public was still strongly in favour of continuing with these agreements (72 per cent in favour, 13 per cent against).[9] When MRBI asked in late May if social partnership had succeed in making Ireland a fairer society a somewhat smaller majority (62 per cent) agreed, with a minority of one out of five disagreeing.[10] This evidence suggests that social partnership is associated in the public's mind more with economic success than with playing a salient role in creating a more equal society.

Key Issues During 2001

The Nice Treaty Referendum

There were two public opinion polls published during the Nice Treaty referendum campaign – both of these were commissioned by *The Irish Times* and undertaken by MRBI.[11] Given the importance of the Treaty there is relatively little survey information on how the campaign developed. This perhaps reflects the general complacency that the referendum would be passed, despite general disinterest in the issue among politicians, the media and electorate.[12] In fact, the way in which respondents were asked how they would vote was not ideal.

The item itself was complicated in asking voting intentions on three topics with a few words describing what each was about. For the Nice Treaty item 'explanation' focused on 'enlargement' as the key theme – this topic was generally the main plank used by the 'yes-side' in its campaign. Given that the Nice Treaty was a complex document, it might have been better if a simple 'how do you intend to vote in the Nice Treaty referendum?' had been asked. The danger, of course, was that many people would simply have replied 'don't know' without some priming. However, given that survey respondents will politely answer questions on which they have no opinion, there is always the danger of eliciting responses which are not the true attitudes of those being interviewed.

Both MRBI polls were undertaken during the final two weeks of May. In the first poll, taken on 14–15 May, there was slender majority support (52 per cent) for the Nice Treaty, with 27 per cent not knowing how (or if?) they would vote and a little over one-fifth (21 per cent) stating they would vote 'no'.[13] Greatest support for the Nice Treaty came from PD supporters (69 per cent), the upper ABC1 social classes (59 per cent) and those living in Connaught-Ulster (59 per cent). In the second poll at the end of May, about one week before the referendum a plurality (45 per cent) declared support for the Treaty. The only groups to show majority support (65 per cent) for the Treaty were Progressive Democrat supporters, who accounted for only three per cent of the electorate. The greatest drop in support was among women, where those saying 'yes' fell from 50 to 40 per cent. The total proportion replying 'don't know' remained constant. In general, the poll evidence suggests that the key features behind the Nice Treaty referendum result were knowledge and voter turnout. We will now look at these features in turn.

The first key feature of the Nice Treaty was the perceived lack of knowledge or information among the electorate. When asked directly how well they understood the issues involved in the Nice Treaty, the proportion claiming to have at least some understanding increased from 37 to 47 per cent. The biggest change came from those who said they had no idea what the treaty was about; their numbers fell from 30 to 19 per cent. Nonetheless, a majority in both polls admitted to not understanding 'the issues involved in the Nice Treaty', so while the campaign made some progress it was never sufficient.

The second key feature of the Nice Treaty result was voter turnout. When asked how likely they were to vote in the referendum, 77 per cent said 'very/fairly likely' with one out of five stating it was 'fairly/very unlikely'. Within the subsequent poll taken some two weeks later these figures did not change, suggesting that the referendum campaign was having no mobilising impact on voters. On polling day, less that 35 percent of voters cast their ballots. Even the polls estimate of those 'very likely' to vote in both polls (56/57 per cent) gave a very inflated estimate of turnout.

During the campaign four aspects of the Nice Treaty were examined by the two MRBI polls. In general, a majority (59 per cent) of the Irish public accepted enlargement of the EU. The public was evenly split over the question of Ireland's participation in a military peacekeeping and enforcement 'Rapid Reaction Force', with half supporting participation and a little under a third favouring an opt out. With regard to the possibility of Ireland losing a commissioner in a twenty-seven member EU there was plurality support (46 per cent) for non-acceptance. Though on the Council question and Ireland's voting weight being cut back in the Council of Ministers the public was almost evenly split with 40 per cent finding the proposal unacceptable and 38 per cent willing to accept it. Not surprisingly, given the complexity of these issues, about one out of five of those interviewed declined to give an opinion.[14]

One other important aspect of the Nice Treaty referendum was the change in attitudes toward integration. Until the final week of the referendum campaign there had always been majority or plurality support for efforts to 'unite fully with the EU' as opposed to Ireland doing all it could to 'protect its independence from the EU'. During the final week support for protecting independence became the plurality view (43 per cent) – the margin between the 'unify' and 'independence' camps was just three points.[15] This marked an important break with the past and was a precursor to the events that unfolded on polling day.

The last published poll taken in 2001, which asked about vote intention in the second Nice Treaty referendum scheduled for late

2002, found that 30 per cent would vote in favour, 27 percent would vote against and the remaining 43 per cent saying they had no opinion (29 per cent) or would not vote (14 per cent). Such results indicated that government hopes for ratifying the Nice Treaty in 2002 would have to be based on a more extensive campaign to educate voters about the treaty and a greater turnout (of 'yes' voters) than that witnessed in 2001.

September 11 and Irish Neutrality

The issue of neutrality emerged on the public agenda twice during 2001, first during the Nice Treaty referendum campaign and later after the terrorist attack on the United States (US) on 11 September. An MRBI question in mid-May asked the public whether or not 'Ireland should continue or discontinue its policy of military neutrality?' An overwhelming majority of 72 per cent favoured continuing this policy with only 16 per cent favouring discontinuance. Support for neutrality was high among all subgroups, but highest among Labour Party supporters (78 per cent).[16]

The events of 11 September could be interpreted as a test of how far the Irish public wished to exercise the principle of neutrality as a policy. Almost two-thirds of those interviewed (63 per cent) felt that allowing the US air force landing and refuelling facilities at Irish airports was a sufficient contribution to the 'war against terrorism'. Nearly one out of ten (9 per cent) favoured doing more, while 18 per cent did not want to 'offer any level of support to the US'.[17]

These results are an interesting example of the 'principle–policy puzzle' within survey research where there is often higher support for a principle but much less support for the application of such a principle in some concrete policy measure, especially where there are costs involved (see Sniderman, Brody and Kuklinski, 1993). More concretely, it seems that about one out of five Irish voters strongly believe in neutrality with about one out of ten of the public favouring the abandonment of neutrality. The majority would seem to favour applying the policy of neutrality on a case-by-case basis.

September 11 and Northern Ireland

It is significant that since the Belfast Agreement (1998) most public opinion poll questions on Northern Ireland relate to the decommissioning of the IRA's weapons. This of course has been one of the key stumbling blocks in the running of the Northern Ireland Assembly. A number of items were asked by IMS in September. The first attempted to see the extent to which the activities of the IRA were seen by the Irish public in the same vein as the 'terrorist attacks on the US' on 11 September. The simple answer to this question is yes. Seven out of ten respondents did not make a distinction between 'the terrorist attacks in the US and those such as the Omagh and Enniskillen bombings'.[18] Nonetheless, for a majority (58 per cent) of the public the events of 11 September did not change their tolerance of the IRA.[19] This apparent inconsistency is an example of a complex feature of public attitudes toward the IRA, which has been noted since the early 1970s, where majorities reject the IRA's use of violence but nonetheless 'understand' the IRA's objectives (see Raven et al., 1976; Davis and Sinnott, 1979).

With regard to IRA decommissioning an overwhelming majority of 85 per cent believed that 'the process of putting its weapons beyond use' should begin.[20] The relatively few questions asked on Northern Ireland and strong majority support for the peace process undertaken with the Belfast Agreement suggests that perhaps the Northern issue is less salient than it once was on the public agenda.[21]

Abortion

The specific issue of abortion came back into the public arena in late 2001 when the Taoiseach announced his party's intention to hold a referendum on the issue before the 2002 general election. Although it was not entirely clear during 2001 that such a referendum would take place IMS nonetheless, in its final poll of the year, asked one question on circumstances in which abortion would be acceptable. It is important to note that the responses to the questions asked on abortion do not readily facilitate estimation of support for a constitutional amendment on abortion, except in estimating core 'pro-life' and 'pro-choice' support.

When asked about the circumstances under which a legal abortion should be available to Irish women, slightly more than one out of five (22 per cent) did not favour abortion under any circumstances, while 12 per cent felt abortion 'should be available without restriction'.[22] The other more limited circumstances for abortion were danger to the mothers life (44 per cent), pregnancy resulting from rape (34 per cent) or incest (28 per cent) or when there was definite evidence of mental/physical disability (11 per cent). The major division on abortion seems to have been on the basis of age, with younger groups more supportive of abortion without restriction and older cohorts favouring not having abortion under any circumstances.

Countdown to the 2002 General Election

In an MRBI poll taken in late May almost one year before the general election, the most important issue for voters was health/hospitals (65 per cent), crime/law and order (40 per cent) and corruption in politics, education and roads traffic (25–6 per cent). An IMS poll in the same month indicated that over three out of four voters were dissatisfied with the health service and a plurality (45 per cent) blamed successive governments for this problem, less blame was placed on those working within the health service (23 per cent) or the current government (21 per cent). As Table 1 shows, all IMS surveys showed health and crime as the key issues with drugs seen as the third most important concern.

However, it is important to be aware here that while the question texts for both polls look the same they were not *implemented* in the same way. MRBI coded respondent replies into precodes, which involved some interpretation of responses by the interviewer. The IMS gave respondents a card showing the issue options considered most relevant, thus priming interviewees to some degree. Furthermore, MRBI gave respondents a choice of picking three issues, while IMS asked for two. The placement of these questions within the surveys was also different. In the MRBI poll

TABLE 1

MOST IMPORTANT ISSUES IN THE NEXT GENERAL ELECTION (PER CENT)

	IMS, 1 Feb. (N=1109)	IMS, 17 May (N=1104)	MRBI, 29–30 May (N=1000)	IMS, 18 Dec. (N=1068)
Health services/hospitals	44	49	65	49
Crime/Law & Order	28	35	40	41
Political corruption	18	18	26	14
Transport/roads/traffic	12	15	25	14
Housing/house prices	25	22	21	13
Drugs	31	30	–	34
Inflation	24	18	–	14
Refugees/asylum seekers	9	7	–	10
Environment/pollution	–	–	–	8
Food/water quality	7	5	–	2
Education	–	–	26	–
Taxation	–	–	17	–
Northern Ireland	–	–	8	–
Quality of life	–	–	8	–
Quality of candidates	–	–	6	–

Sources: MRBI/5593/01, 29–30 May, question 1, 'In the next general election, what are the three most important issues which will influence the way you vote?' IMS: EW/MOF/NN/115S1, 1 Feb., q.13; EW/NN/MOF/317S1, 17 May, q.10; EW/CF/NN/698S1, 18 Dec., q. 11; SHOW CARD B 'If there were to be a general election in the next six months which one of the following issues would have most influence on how you would vote? And which would be the second most influential?' [First and second issues].

the issue question was the first item asked, while in the IMS surveys it occurred in the middle of the interview after respondents had answered party and leadership support questions. These methodological differences may explain some of the differences between the poll results.

When it came to the formation of the next government the most preferred coalition was Fianna Fáil/PDs and Independents (38 per cent) – 25 percentage points more popular than the next option, a Fianna Fáil/Labour partnership. One of the newsworthy concerns among many political commentators was the impact that Sinn Féin might have in the 2002 general election. The public was almost evenly split on the implicit 'acceptability' (whatever that might mean?) of 'Sinn Féin as part of the next coalition government' with 47 per cent saying they would accept it and 41 per cent saying they would not. Significantly, when the IMS asked the same question in late September they used a much more strident wording relating to the acceptability of Sinn Féin government ministers getting into office by holding the balance of power in a 'hung Dáil' if there was no 'evidence of IRA decommissioning'. With this item, a plurality (45 per cent) said they did not want Sinn Féin ministers while 37 per cent were willing to accept this hypothetical situation.[23]

One of the most extensive time-series within Irish public opinion polls is that on party support. However, there have been very few questions asked on what the Irish public thinks of political parties beyond vote intention, satisfaction with leader and ability to deal with various issues such as the economy and Northern Ireland. Given the revelations of the various tribunals of inquiry since 1997 the IMS asked in late 2001 what voters thought of political parties more generally.[24] This 'party image' question is less than satisfactory because the item is ambiguous. Respondents could have expressed what they thought was the prevailing opinion on parties as depicted in the media. Alternatively, those interviewed may have expressed their own personal opinion. In addition, many of the scores for parties are very close to first preference intentions (including don't knows) in the same survey.

Given these caveats, the item does indicate that 39 per cent of Fianna Fáil's own supporters thought that the party is the 'most politically corrupt'. Furthermore, Irish voters, especially supporters of the smaller parties, seem willing to endorse positive attributes such as 'best at getting things done' to other parties and more particularly Fianna Fáil. For example, only half of all Fine Gael identifiers stated that Fine Gael was best in this respect while over three-quarters of Fianna Fáil supporters stuck with their party. In fact, 17 per cent of Fine Gael voters believed that Fianna Fáil was best at getting things done. What this really tells us about party image in Ireland is difficult to say; more concrete evidence will have to wait for the results of future research such as the first Irish National Election Study.

Conclusion

This brief overview of poll results for 2001 indicates that many of the key features of the 2002 contest were in place up to a year before polling day. In the last full year before the general election Fianna Fáil remained the most popular party, while the ratings for the Taoiseach and government indicated a high level of public satisfaction. Concerns about health and crime seemed set to be the key campaign issues in 2002. Attitudes toward the Nice Treaty remained ambiguous, even after its defeat in June, and left open the question of how the government would undertake a second campaign in the autumn of 2002.

Acknowledgements

Thanks to Fiachra Kennedy for constructive comments; the usual disclaimer applies.

Notes

1. A ninth survey released to the public in 2001 was carried out by IMS between 20 August and 10 September for the European Commission Representation in Ireland with a quota sample of 1,245 adults. The results were released to the public in the form of a report written by Professor Richard Sinnott of UCD. This report is available at <http://www.euireland.ie/news/Institutions/1001/fullopinionpollresults.pdf>.
2. Satisfaction with the Fine Gael leader was 60 per cent in July 1997 and had fallen to 29 per cent by the 2002 general election. The pattern in 2001 followed this general trend.
3. The most reliable data on government satisfaction in Ireland go back to 1979. Looking at a quarterly representation of data for this whole period there would appear to be no previous example of such an increase in satisfaction over a year – though there have been examples of decline in satisfaction of this magnitude in 1992–1993.
4. MRBI/5444/01, 14–15 January 2001, question 8, 'Do you think that your standard of living will rise; fall or remain the same as a result of the budget? (1) Will rise (2) Will fall (3) Will stay the same (4) No opinion.'
5. MRBI/5444/01, 14–15 January 2001, question 8a 'In your opinion, was this budget good for the country or bad for the country? (1) Good for the country (2) Bad for the country (3) No opinion.'
6. MRBI/5577/01, 14–15 May 2001, question 6, 'There has been some discussion about the role that social partnership between government, employers, unions, farmers and voluntary organisations has played in our prosperity. In your view, should social partnership continue, or not? (1) Yes (2) No (3) No opinion.'; question 6a 'And has social partnership, or has it not, succeeded in making this a fairer society? (1) Yes (2) No (3) No opinion.'
7. IMS: EW/CF/NN/698S1, 18 December 2001, question 17, 'Following strong growth in recent years, the economy has now suffered a slow down. How long do you think

the current slowdown will continue for? Will it last … READ OUT (1) Less than a year (2) A year (3) Two years (4) 3-4 years (5) 5 years or longer (6) Don't know/no opinion'.

8. IMS: EW/CF/NN/698S1, 18 December 2001, question 17, 'Taking everything into consideration would you say that your standard of living has improved, disimproved or remained the same over the last 12 months? (1) Improved (2) Disimproved (3) Remained the same (4) Don't know/no opinion.'

9. MRBI/5593/01, 29–30 May 2001, question 6 'There has been some discussion about the role that social partnership between government, employers, unions, farmers and voluntary organisations has played in our prosperity. In your view, should social partnership continue, or not? [Yes, no or no opinion].'

10. MRBI/5593/01, 29–30 May 2001, question 6a 'And has social partnership, or has it not, succeeded in making this a fairer society? [Yes, no or no opinion].'

11. There were items on the other two referendums on the accession to the International Criminal Court and abolition of the death penalty. These issues were relatively uncontroversial, if not equally bewildering to the electorate, and will not be examined in this report.

12. For a more detailed overview of the Nice Treaty campaign see O' Mahony, 2001.

13. MRBI/5577/01, 14–15 May 2001, question 7, 'As you may know, three Referendums are being held on June 7th next on a number of issues. For each of the Referendums shown on this card, I would like you to tell whether you are likely to Yes or No [or No opinion] ? SHOW CARD. (a) The Nice Treaty which provides, among other things, for enlargement of the number of countries in the European Union…'

14. MRBI/5593/01, 14–15 May, question 10, 'Now we'd like to ask your opinion about some aspects of the Nice Treaty. (d) The EU has established the military reaction Rapid Reaction Force for humanitarian tasks, peacekeeping and peace-making. Do you think that … (1) Ireland should participate in the Rapid Reaction Force (2) Ireland should negotiate to opt out from participating in the Rapid Reaction Force (3) No opinion'. This item was also asked again in MRBI/5577/01, 29–30 May 2001, question 8(e). MRBI/5593/01, question 11 'To prepare for enlarging the number of states in the EU from 15 to 27 or more, the Nice Treaty proposes some changes in its decision-making procedures. I would like to ask you whether you think the following changes as they affect Ireland, are acceptable or unacceptable? SHOW CARD (a) When the number of member states reaches 27, the right of each state to have a Commissioner will rotate so that there will be limited periods when Ireland (& each country in turn) will have no Commissioner. (b) Ireland's share of the votes in the EU Council of Ministers will be reduced from 3.45 per cent of the votes in a Union of 15 members to 2.02 per cent in a Union of 27 members.' MRBI/5577/01, question 8 'Now we'd like to ask your opinion about some aspects of the Nice Treaty. (d) The European Union proposes to admit up to 13 new member states over the next 10 years. Are you in favour or against enlargement of the EU in this way'.

15. MRBI/5593/01, 14–15 May 2001, question 8c 'Which of the following statements comes closest to your view of Ireland's status within the EU? SHOW CARD (1) Ireland should do all it can to unite fully with the EU (2) Ireland should do all it can to protect its independence from the EU (3) No opinion/don't know.' This item was also asked again in MRBI/5577/01, 29–30 May 2001, question 10c.

16. MRBI/5593/01, 14–15 May 2001, question 8 'Now we'd like to ask your opinion about some aspects of the Nice Treaty. (f) Do you think that Ireland should continue or discontinue its policy of military neutrality? [Continue, Discontinue, No opinion]'.

17. IMS: EW/CF/NN/567S1, 27 September 2001, question 14 'The Irish government has offered the US landing and refuelling facilities at Irish airports in the ward against international terrorism. Which of the following best describes your own opinion? READ OUT (1) Allowing the US to land and refuel at Irish airports is the appropriate level of support for Ireland to offer (2) Ireland should support the US in a more

significant way by participating in military action with the US and its allies (3) Ireland should not offer any level of support at all to the US (4) Don't know/no opinion.'

18. IMS: EW/CF/NN/567S1, 27 September 2001, question 19 'Leaving aside the difference in scale of the attacks, do you personally make any distinction or not between the terrorist acts in the US and those such as the Omagh and Enniskillen bombings in Northern Ireland? (1) Yes, make a distinction (2) No, do not make a distinction (3) Don't know/no opinion'.

19. IMS: EW/CF/NN/567S1, 27 September 2001, question 18 'Are you more or less tolerant now of the IRA following the terrorist attacks on the US, or is there no change in your attitude? (1) More tolerant (2) Less tolerant (3) Hasn't changed my attitude (4) Don't know/no opinion.'

20. IMS: EW/CF/NN/567S1, 27 September 2001, question 20 'Do you or do you not, believe the IRA should now begin the process of putting its weapons beyond use? (1) Should begin (2) Should not begin (3) Don't know/no opinion.'

21. Note that in MRBI/5444/01, 22–3 January 2001, question 17, a majority (55 per cent) supported nationalists joining the new Northern Ireland Police Service. However, 15 per cent were against and 30 per cent expressed no opinion.

22. IMS: EW/CF/NN/698S1, 18 December 2001, question 22, SHOW CARD E 'The subject of abortion is being debated again, with the likelihood of a referendum at some stage in 2002. In what circumstances, if any, do you yourself believe that legal abortion should be available to Irish women? (1) In no circumstances (2) Where the mothers life is in danger (3) Where there is a risk of suicide (4) Where pregnancy results from rape (5) Where pregnancy results from incest (6) Where there is definite evidence of physical or mental disability in the unborn child (7) Should be available without restriction (8) Don't know/no opinion.'

23. The question text for the MRBI/5593/01, 29–30 May 2001, question 4(a), was 'Most observers believe that the outcome of the next general election will lead to the formation of another coalition government. If this were to happen, which of these coalition options would you prefer? ... [five options given, none of which included SF – plus a 'none of the above'] ... (a) Would you or would you not accept Sinn Féin as part of the next coalition government [yes, no or don't know]'. The question text for the IMS: EW/CF/NN/567S1, 27 September 2001, question 9, was 'If the next general election in the Republic results in a hung Dáil, where Sinn Féin holds the balance of power, do you think that Sinn Féin ministers should be included in any coalition government formed, even if there is no evidence of IRA decommissioning? [yes, no or don't know]'.

24. IMS: EW/CF/NN698S1, 18 December 2001, question 12 'I am now going to read you out some words and phrases that some people have used to describe political parties in Ireland. For each description please tell me which political party you feel the description applies to most?' (1) Best at getting things done (2) Most in touch with the people (3) The most visionary (4) Most politically corrupt. [FF, FG, Lab., PD, Sinn Féin, Greens, Independents, None, Don't know].

References

Davis, E.E. and R. Sinnott. 1979. *Attitudes in the Republic of Ireland Relevant to the Northern Ireland Problem* (Dublin: ESRI Paper No.97).

Jones, Jack. 2001. *In Your Opinion: Political and Social Trends in Ireland Through the Eyes of the Electorate*. Dublin: Town House.

O'Mahoney, Jane. 2001. 'Not So Nice: The Treaty of Nice, the International Criminal Court, the Abolition of the Death Penalty – The 2001 Referendum Experience'. *Irish Political Studies* 16, pp.201–14.

Raven, John, C.T. Whelan, P. Pfretzschner and D. Borock. 1976. *Political Culture in Ireland: The views of Two Generations* (Dublin: IPA).

Sniderman, Paul M., Richard A. Brody and James H. Kuklinski. 1993. 'The Principle–Policy Puzzle: The Paradox of American Racial Attitudes', in Paul M. Sniderman, Richard A. Bordy and Phillip E. Tetlock, eds, *Reasoning and Choice: Explorations in Political Psychology* (Cambridge: Cambridge University Press), pp.58–69.

PAT LYONS currently works as a researcher in the Public Opinion and Political Behaviour Research Programme, at the Institute for the Study of Social Change, University College Dublin. He is a PhD candidate at the Department of Political Science, Trinity College Dublin. His main areas of research are public opinion in Ireland, attitudes toward European integration and political participation.

REPUBLIC OF IRELAND

1. Government Ministers, Ministers of State and Opposition Spokespersons (September 2001)

TABLE 1.1

GOVERNMENT MINISTERS AND OPPOSITION SPOKESPERSONS

Position	Government	Fine Gael
Taoiseach	Bertie Ahern	Michael Noonan
Tanaiste and Minister for Enterprise, Trade and Employment	Mary Harney	Charles Flanagan and Deirdre Clune
Education and Science	Michael Woods	Michael Creed
Public Enterprise	Mary O'Rourke	Jim Higgins
Defence	Michael Smith	Alan Shatter
Agriculture, Food and Rural Development	Joe Walsh	Alan Dukes
Finance	Charlie McCreevy	Jim Mitchell
Foreign Affairs	Brian Cowen	Jim O'Keeffe
Environment and Local Government	Noel Dempsey	Deirdre Clune and Olivia Mitchell
Social, Community and Family Affairs	Dermot Ahern	Brian Hayes
Arts, Heritage, Gaeltacht and the Islands	Sile de Valera	Dinny McGinley
Justice, Equality and Law Reform	John O'Donoghue	Alan Shatter
Tourism, Sport and Recreation	Jim McDaid	Jim Higgins and Michael Creed
Health and Children	Micheál Martin	Gay Mitchell and Frances Fitzgerald
Marine and Natural Resources	Frank Fahey	Alan Dukes
Attorney General	Michael McDowell	

Sources: Government: Administration Yearbook and Diary, 2002, IPA; Fine Gael: Fine Gael Press Office.

TABLE 1.2

MINISTERS OF STATE

Minister of State	Department (Special Responsibilities)
Seamus Brennan	Taoiseach (Government Chief Whip) and Defence
Bobby Molloy	Government and Environment and Local Government (Housing and Urban Renewal)
Noel Davern	Agriculture, Food and Rural Development (Livestock Breeding, Horticulture and Food)
Noel Treacy	Education and Science and Enterprise, Trade and Employment (Science and Technology)
Joe Jacob	Public Enterprise (Energy)
Willie O'Dea	Education and Science (Adult Education, Youth Affairs and School Transport)
Tom Kitt	Enterprise, Trade and Employment (Labour affairs, Consumer Rights and International Trade)
Danny Wallace	Environment and Local Government (Environmental Information and Awareness and the Environmental Protection Agency)
Hugh Byrne	Marine and Natural Resources (Aquaculture and Forestry)
Mary Wallace	Justice, Equality and Law Reform (Equality and Disabilities)
Martin Cullen	Finance (Office of Public Works)
Eamon O Cuiv	Agriculture, Food and Rural Development (Rural Development and the Western Development Commission)
Liz O'Donnell	Foreign Affairs (Overseas Development Assistance and Human Rights)
Tom Moffatt	Health and Children (Food Safety and Older People)
Eoin Ryan	Tourism, Sport and Recreation (Local Development and National Drugs Strategy Team)
Mary Hanafin	Justice, Equality and Law Reform and Education and Science (Children)
Mary Coughlan	Arts, Heritage, Gaeltacht and Islands (Gaeltacht and Islands)

Source: Administration Yearbook and Diary, 2002, IPA.

2. State of the Parties (September 2001)

TABLE 2.1

STATE OF THE PARTIES

Party	Number of Seats	Ceann Comhairle
Fianna Fail	75	
Fine Gael	54	
Labour	21	Seamus Pattison
Progressive Democrats	4	
Greens	2	
Sinn Féin	1	
Socialist Party	1	
Others	8	

Source: Administration Yearbook and Diary, 2002, IPA.

3. Oirechtas Committees

TABLE 3.1

DÁIL COMMITTEES

Committee	Chair
Public Accounts	Michael Finucane
Members' Interests	Tony Killeen
Procedures and Privileges	Seamus Pattison

Source: Administration Yearbook and Diary, 2002, IPA.

TABLE 3.2

JOINT COMMITTEES

Committee	Chair
Agriculture, Food and Marine	John Browne
Broadcasting and Parliamentary Information	Seamus Brennan
Consolidation Bills	Michael Ahern
Education and Science	Michael P Kitt
Enterprise and Small Business	Ivor Callely
Environment and Local Government	Jackie Healy-Rae
European Affairs	Bernard Durkan
Family, Community and Social Affairs	Noel Ahern
Finance and Public Service	Michael Ahern
Foreign Affairs	Desmond J O Malley
Health and Children	Batt O'Keeffe
Heritage and the Irish Language	Donal Carey
Justice, Equality, Defence and Women's Rights	Sean Ardagh
Public Enterprise and Transport	Sean Doherty
Strategic Management Initiative	Dick Roche
Tourism, Sport and Recreation	Breeda Moynihan-Cronin
Joint House Services Committee	Ben Briscoe
All-Party Oireachtas Committee on the Constitution	Brian Lenihan

Source: Administration Yearbook and Diary, 2002, IPA

TABLE 3.3

SEANAD COMMITTEES

Committee	Chair
Seanad Committee of Selection	Liam T Cosgrave
Members' Interests	Brian Mullooly
Procedures and Privileges	Brian Mullooly

Source: Administration Yearbook and Diary, 2002, IPA

TABLE 3.4

SUB-COMMITTEES

Committee	Chair
Dáil Reform	Seamus Brennan
Members' Services (Dáil)	Tony Killeen
Members' Services (Seanad)	Donie Cassidy

Source: Administration Yearbook and Diary, 2002, IPA.

4. Bills Enacted by the Oireachtas (2001)

Full Titles and Acts are available at <http://www.gov.ie/oireachtas> and <http://www.ucc.ie/law/irlii/2001statutes.htm>.

1. Aviation Regulation Act, 2001. [21 February 2001]
2. Customs and Excise (Mutual Assistance) Act, 2001. [9 March 2001]
3. Diseases of Animals (Amendment) Act, 2001. [9 March 2001]
4. Broadcasting Act, 2001. [14 March 2001]
5. Social Welfare Act, 2001. [23 March 2001]
6. Trustee Savings Banks (Amendment) Act, 2001. [28 March 2001]
7. Finance Act, 2001. [30 March 2001]
8. Teaching Council Act, 2001. [17 April 2001]
9. Electricity (Supply) (Amendment) Act, 2001. [17 April 2001]
10. Housing (Gaeltacht) (Amendment) Act, 2001. [23 April 2001]
11. Industrial Relations (Amendment) Act, 2001. [29 May 2001]
12. ACC Bank Act, 2001. [29 May 2001]
13. Valuation Act, 2001. [4 June 2001]
14. Health (Miscellaneous Provisions) Act, 2001. [5 June 2001]
15. Irish Nationality and Citizenship Act, 2001. [5 June 2001]
16. Euro Changeover (Amounts) Act, 2001. [25 June 2001]
17. Health Insurance (Amendment) Act, 2001. [27 June 2001]
18. Sex Offenders Act, 2001. [30 June 2001]
19. Carer's Leave Act, 2001. [2 July 2001]
20. Horse and Greyhound Racing Act, 2001. [2 July 2001]
21. Nitrigin Eireann Teoranta Act, 2001. [3 July 2001]
22. Motor Vehicle (Duties and Licences) Act, 2001. [3 July 2001]
23. Vocational Education (Amendment) Act, 2001. [5 July 2001]
24. Children Act, 2001. [8 July 2001]
25. Mental Health Act, 2001. [8 July 2001]
26. Irish National Petroleum Corporation Limited Act, 2001. [9 July 2001]
27. Prevention of Corruption (Amendment) Act, 2001. [9 July 2001]
28. Company Law Enforcement Act, 2001. [9 July 2001]
29. Agriculture Appeals Act, 2001. [9 July 2001]
30. Oireachtas (Ministerial and Parliamentary Offices) (Amendment) Act, 2001. [14 July 2001]
31. Standards in Public Office Act, 2001[14 July 2001]
32. Dormant Accounts Act, 2001[14 July 2001]
33. Ministerial, Parliamentary and Judicial Offices and Oireachtas Members (Miscellaneous Provisions) Act, 2001. [16 July 2001]
34. Adventure Activities Standards Authority Act, 2001. [16 July 2001]
35. Human Rights Commission (Amendment) Act, 2001. [16 July 2001]
36. Waste Management (Amendment) Act, 2001. [17 July 2001]

37. Local Government Act, 2001. [21st July 2001]
38. Electoral (Amendment) Act, 2001. [24 October 2001]
39. Industrial Designs Act, 2001. [27 November 2001]
40. Fisheries (Amendment) Act, 2001. [27 November 2001]
41. European Communities and Swiss Confederation Act, 2001. [1st December 2001]
42. Youth Work Act, 2001. [1st December 2001]
43. Ordnance Survey Ireland Act, 2001. [5 December 2001]
44. Heritage Fund Act, 2001. [10 December 2001]
45. Protection of Employees (Part-Time Work) Act, 2001. [15 December 2001]
46. Horse Racing Ireland (Membership) Act, 2001. [18 December 2001]
47. Asset Covered Securities Act, 2001. [18 December 2001]
48. Air Navigation and Transport (Indemnities) Act, 2001. [19 December 2001]
49. Extradition (European Union Conventions) Act, 2001. [19 December 2001]
50. Criminal Justice (Theft and Fraud Offences) Act, 2001. [19 December 2001]
51. Social Welfare (No. 2) Act, 2001. [20 December 2001]
52. Appropriation Act, 2001. [20 December 2001]
53. Referendum Act, 2001 . [22 December 2001]
54. Family Support Agency Act, 2001. [22 December 2001]
55. Transport (Railway Infrastructure) Act, 2001. [23 December 2001]

5. Main Political Events of 2001

January

1   UN: Ireland became a member of the UN Security Council for a two-year term. Ireland was elected on 10 October 2000 to serve as one of ten non-permanent members of the Security Council.
8   Lawlor: Contempt proceedings against Dublin West TD Liam Lawlor opened in the High Court. Proceedings were initiated by counsel for the Flood tribunal in December after its chairman, Mr Justice Fergus Flood, stood down Mr Lawlor as a witness, saying it was clear he had failed to comply with a High Court order to provide the tribunal with records and documents. On 9 January an application to the High Court judge, Mr Justice Thomas Smyth, that he discharge himself from the case and assign it to another judge was turned down.
10 Haughey: The former Taoiseach, Mr Charles Haughey, dropped legal challenges to a ruling that he must continue to testify to the Moriarty tribunal in spite of poor health. He resumed giving evidence in private in a room in Dublin Castle.
11 Lawlor: Liam Lawlor was forced to resign as vice-chairman of an Oireachtas Finance and Public Service Committee when Senator John Dardis (Progressive Democrat) indicated he would vote no confidence in Lawlor.
11 Election: Fine Gael, the Labour Party and the Green Party told all party officers and administrative staff they are on alert for an election. No holiday leave granted for May and June.
17 Lawlor: Liam Lawlor becomes the first politician to be jailed as a result of investigations by a tribunal. The Taoiseach condemns Lawlor's behaviour towards the Flood tribunal and agrees to remove him from Dáil committees. In a letter to the Fine Gael leader, John Bruton, the Taoiseach said that the Government would table a motion calling on Lawlor to resign his Dáil seat if he failed to co-operate fully with the Flood tribunal (19 January).
20 Lawlor: The Flood Tribunal announced that it would investigate whether Lawlor destroyed documents he had been ordered to give to the tribunal.
22 Party Funding: Ivan Yates (Fine Gael) said there was no question of the party returning a £50,000 donation made by Mr Denis O'Brien, as the money had already been spent.
22 EU: The European Commission recommended that Ireland should be formally censured for pursuing economic policies inconsistent with agreed European guidelines.

21

25 **EU:** The Minister for Finance, Charlie McCreevy accused Ireland's European critics of being jealous of the State's economic success and insisted that he will not be rewriting his Budget. McCreevy said there have been some 'green eyes' cast upon the prosperity of the Irish economy and that the State's success in securing low rates of corporation tax to attract foreign investment was a particular bone of contention for other member-states.

26 **Fine Gael:** Opponents of the Fine Gael leader, John Bruton, urged potential alternative candidates to support another challenge to his position after an *Irish Times*/MRBI opinion poll showed a further drop in his and his party's support.

29 **Fine Gael:** Two former cabinet ministers, Michael Noonan and Jim Mitchell, launched a campaign to oust Bruton.

30 **TD's Pay:** The Government accepted proposals for an increase in TDs' salaries of 19 per cent which brought the annual pay of a TD up from £39,000 to £46,500. Ministers' salaries were brought above the £100,000 mark for the first time.

30 **Lawlor:** A Government motion calling on Liam Lawlor to fully meet the requirements of the courts and the Flood tribunal or voluntarily resign his membership of the Dáil was passed by 79 votes to 72.

31 **Fine Gael:** John Bruton removed as leader of Fine Gael.

February

1 **Lindsay Tribunal:** Judge Alison Lindsay, chairwoman of the haemophilia tribunal, ruled that hospitals, health boards and other parties before the tribunal are entitled to claim privilege over certain documents.

9 **Fine Gael:** Michael Noonan defeated Enda Kenny by 44 votes to 28 to become leader of Fine Gael. Mr Michael Noonan ends Fine Gael's dependence on corporate funding.

12 **EU:** At a meeting of EU finance ministers in Brussels Charlie McCreevy defended his economic policies.

15 **Fine Gael:** New front bench announced with Enda Kenny demoted to back-benches.

17 **O'Keeffe:** Ned O'Keeffe, Minister of State at the Department of Agriculture, resigned because of a decision by the Public Offices Commission to investigate (under the Ethics in Public Office Act) concerns over his non-disclosure of his family farm's licence to feed meat-and-bonemeal to pigs. On 19 February Mary Coughlan was promoted in a minor reshuffle following the resignation of O'Keeffe

21 **Foot and Mouth:** Department of Agriculture inspectors carried out an intensive investigation in the Virginia area of Co Cavan, after animals were delivered on a lorry which had earlier transported livestock to the British abattoir where foot-and-mouth disease had been confirmed.

21 **Burke:** Ray Burke began his evidence to the Flood tribunal in relation to his dealings with Century Radio. The tribunal investigated the payment of £35,000 to Burke by Century's co-founder, Oliver Barry.

21 **Lindsay Tribunal:** The Irish Haemophilia Society reacted angrily to the decision of the Irish Blood Transfusion Service not to waive privilege over confidential documents relating to the 1991 financial settlement with HIV-infected victims of contaminated blood products.

23 **Foot and Mouth:** A five-mile exclusion zone was placed around a mid-Ulster farm on which a dead cow displayed symptoms of foot-and-mouth disease. On 26 February, all marts in the Republic of Ireland were suspended. On 27 February, the Government convened a top-level group to co-ordinate the day-to-day management of the foot-and-mouth crisis. All GAA games as well as major rugby, soccer and equestrian events were cancelled. Urban dwellers were asked to stay out of the countryside to minimise the risk of a foot-and-mouth outbreak in the Republic.

26 **Nice Treaty:** European Union foreign ministers signed the Treaty of Nice, putting into legal form the agreement reached at December's summit.

March

1 **Dual Mandate:** Four Independent TDs turned down the Government's offer to compromise on legislation designed to ban Oireachtas members from holding local authority seats.

5 **Party Funding:** Fine Gael declined to confirm or deny that it received a donation of £50,000 from Denis O'Brien at about the time the former chief executive of Esat Digifone successfully bid for a mobile telephone licence.

9 **ASTI:** Secondary teachers reacted furiously to a Labour Court recommendation on their 30 per cent claim and threatened to disrupt the Leaving and Junior Certificate exams. The court made no 'upfront' pay offer to the ASTI, asking it instead to pursue its case through the Government's new bench marking pay body.

12 **Party Funding:** The Government withdrew its offer to abandon spending limit increases in the next general election after Labour refused to join an all-party review of political party funding.

19 **ASTI:** Secondary teachers ruled out placing pickets on exam centres in the event that their dispute with the Government remaining unresolved.

19 **Haughey:** The former Taoiseach, Charles Haughey, was still 'critically ill, but stable' in hospital in Dublin following a collapse at his home

20 **Foot and Mouth:** Precautionary restrictions were placed on a farm in Co Louth. On 22 March 10,000 sheep and 2,500 cattle were slaughtered in an attempt to prevent the spread of the first confirmed outbreak of foot-and-mouth disease in the State in nearly 60 years.

23 **Cooper-Flynn:** Beverley Cooper-Flynn failed to win damages in her libel case against RTÉ and other defendants. A High Court jury found that RTÉ had failed to prove the TD induced a retired farmer, James Howard, to evade tax by ignoring the 1993 tax amnesty. But the jury found RTÉ had proved Cooper-Flynn advised or encouraged other named persons to evade tax. The jury said that, in light of this finding, Cooper-Flynn's reputation had not suffered material injury.

28 **ASTI:** The Association of Secondary Teachers Ireland lifted its ban on supervising and correcting exams as new Labour Court proposals emerged.

30 **SSIA:** According to documents released under the Freedom of Information Act, the Minister for Finance, Charlie McCreevy, went against the advice of his officials when he introduced the scheme in February.

April

2 **Lawlor:** The High Court was told that Liam Lawlor had not provided the Flood tribunal with all the documents it sought by the deadline of 30 March (fixed by Mr Justice Smyth when he jailed Lawlor for seven days for failing to co-operate with the tribunal).

3 **Redmond:** The former assistant Dublin city and county manager, George Redmond, appeared in Dublin District Court on corruption charges relating to land transactions in west Dublin.

4 **Sinn Féin:** A report on Sinn Féin activity in so-called 'crime-solving' in north Kerry was presented to the Minister for Justice, John O'Donoghue. The Minister ordered the report following revelations in early March that Sinn Féin activists were investigating a spate of thefts in north Kerry and were in some cases returning property to its rightful owners.

10 **Arms Trial:** An RTÉ Prime Time programme produced documentation that showed that 16 alterations had been made to a statement by the then head of military intelligence Col Hefferon before it was forwarded to the attorney general, Mr Colm Condon, for inclusion in the book of evidence in advance of the Arms Trial in 1970. According to the programme the changes were almost certainly made within the Department of Justice, where Des O'Malley had just been appointed minister by the

then Taoiseach, Jack Lynch. The original statement carried an official Department of Justice stamp and the initials of Peter Berry, secretary of the Department. It carried notations in the margin in Berry's hand. The sections dealt with in this way were subsequently removed. The former leader of the Progressive Democrats, O'Malley, had no recollection of a statement made by a former Col Michael Hefferon.

10　**Cooper-Flynn:** Beverley Cooper-Flynn refused to attend a meeting to discuss her future with senior party figures.

11　**Cooper-Flynn:** Beverley Cooper-Flynn was expelled from the Fianna Fáil parliamentary party after the Taoiseach insisted her continued presence was damaging.

12　**Arms Trial:** According to a document signed by Des O'Malley under his official ministerial seal the then Minister for Justice 'examined and considered' the file before directing that privilege be claimed for it and its contents on 7 October 1970. The Department of Justice made the signed and sealed certificate of privilege available through the National Archives under the 30-year rule.

13　**Arms Trial:** Des O'Malley pledged to co-operate with any inquiry into the arms trial, saying it should examine all aspects of the trial and the events leading up to it.

15　**Arms Trial:** The judge who presided over the arms trial, Seamus Henchy, a former Supreme Court judge, said he had not been aware that a file containing a key statement was withheld from the 1970 trial.

19　**ASTI:** Teachers rejected the Labour Court pay offer and set in train a new programme of industrial action.

19　**Arms Trial:** According to documents released at the Public Record Office in London the testimony of the then Minister for Defence, Jim Gibbons, at the 1970 Arms Trial, meant that the Taoiseach, Jack Lynch, thought he might have to sack him.

23　**Arms Trial:** According to personal statements prepared by Jack Lynch in 1980 (10 years after the arms trial and a few months after he resigned as Taoiseach) the first time he knew of 'any alleged involvement of my Ministers' in an attempt to import arms was on Monday, 20 April 1970. Jack Lynch's private papers are not government records because they fall outside his period in office. They were entrusted by an official in the Taoiseach's Department to Dr Martin Mansergh for Fianna Fáil. Mrs Lynch and the Taoiseach, Mr Ahern, agreed to release them to the *Irish Times*, believing that they belonged to the public record.

27　**Abbeylara:** Nine members of the Garda Emergency Response Unit sought exemptions from giving evidence to an Oireachtas subcommittee inquiry into the Abbeylara shooting.

27　**SSIA:** In the High Court, Denis Riordan, challenged the introduction of the Government's new Special Savings Scheme.

29　**Arms Trial:** In the first of a four-part RTÉ series, *Des O'Malley – A Public Life*, O'Malley denied altering, or approving or directing anyone else to alter, the statement of Col Michael Hefferon in the 1970 Arms Trial. Neither could he remember directing that privilege should attach to a file containing that statement. He called for a full inquiry as he did not want an inquiry into one aspect only, because it was a very complex affair and a lot of material that had not been given to the arms trial could now be made available. O'Malley said he had no reason to believe Jack Lynch's reputation would be affected as it was Jack Lynch and himself and several other ministers who had stood in the breach to prevent the country being led towards a civil war. Later in the year, 5 July, the Minister for Justice, John O'Donoghue, and the Attorney General, Michael McDowell, concluded that claims of a conspiracy to suppress vital Arms Trial evidence in 1970 were unlikely to be true.

30　**Abbeylara:** The inquiry into the fatal shooting of John Carthy by two ERU members on 20 April 2000, was adjourned until at least 1 June.

May

1　**Foot and Mouth:** Dublin Zoo opened and hill-walking, pony trekking and angling can resume from 11 May.

2 The referendum on judicial accountability was dropped because the government and opposition failed to reach agreement on the matter. The main amendments concerned the reduction from 30 to 20 of the number of members of either the Oireachtas or Seanad needed to sign a motion initiating a motion of impeachment and that a simple majority, rather than a two-thirds majority, as originally proposed, would be necessary.

3 **Lowry:** RTÉ news reported that former Fine Gael minister, Michael Lowry, would be questioned by the Moriarty tribunal about £150,000 allegedly lodged in an offshore bank account while he was minister for communications.

5 **Election:** Taoiseach told Fianna Fáil TDs and possible candidates to increase their profiles in their constituencies over the summer months. However, the Government strongly rejected suggestions that this should be taken as a hint that a summer general election was on the cards.

5 The Minister for Foreign Affairs, Brian Cowen, was hit by a motorcyclist as he crossed the road from St Stephen's Green to his office in Iveagh House.

8 **Phone Tapping:** Former minister Martin O'Donoghue alleged he was told by fellow minister George Colley that the telephones of a number of people in the 1982 Cabinet were tapped. Des O'Malley, said the head of the IDA, Michael Killeen, had delivered a similar warning to him when he came to his home. The handwritten note passed on by Mr Killeen, which allegedly emerged from within the Garda Síochána, declared that O'Malley's telephone and those of other ministers had been tapped.

8 The Cabinet agreed a reshuffle of ambassadorial posts, including the appointment of Ann Anderson as Ireland's Permanent Representative to the EU.

8 **Fine Gael:** The deputy leader of Fine Gael, Jim Mitchell, was cleared of any wrongdoing by the Public Offices Commission in relation to an opinion poll conducted into the party leadership in January (the poll had found he was the first choice of voters to succeed Mr John Bruton as leader).

9 **Nice Treaty:** Government launched the referendum campaign.

11 **Fine Gael:** Fine Gael admited giving £120,000 in illegal under-the-counter cash payments to its staff over a nine-year period,

13 The Dean of St Patrick's Cathedral in Dublin, the Very Rev. Robert MacCarthy, declined an invitation to a State reception honouring Cardinal Connell in Dublin Castle. He said he was doing so 'on principle' as it was his practice to do so when he received invitations 'in the name of the Taoiseach and Ms Larkin'.

14 **Health:** The Minister for Finance, Charlie McCreevy, said that the Department of Health would have to join the queue when it comes to demanding extra funding in the budget. Ministers met in Ballymascanlon, Co. Louth, to discuss the crisis in the health services.

14 Cardinal Connell was welcomed at a state reception in his honour held at Dublin Castle by the Taoiseach and the Tánaiste. Celia Larkin, who co-hosted the reception, was not in the welcoming party nor was she mentioned by Dr Connell in his address.

14 **Abbeylara:** The Labour Party leader, Ruairí Quinn, said that the internal Garda investigation into the death of John Carthy in Abbeylara would not meet European human rights standards.

16 **Fine Gael:** Michael Noonan told members of the Fine Gael parliamentary party yesterday he would investigate illegal 'under-the-counter' payments to party staff and report to them on the findings.

18 The Provisional IRA chief-of-staff from 1969 to 1972, Seán Mac Stiofáin, died aged 73.

21 **Nice Treaty:** Michael Noonan challenged the Tánaiste, Mary Harney, the Minister for Finance, Charlie McCreevy, and the Minister for Arts, Heritage, Gaeltacht and the Islands, Sile de Valera, whom he described as 'the eurosceptics in Cabinet', to play a leading role in the drive for a yes vote on the Treaty of Nice.

21 **Abbeylara:** Thirty-six gardaí were given leave by the High Court to challenge the Oireachtas sub-committee inquiry into the shooting dead of John Carthy in Abbeylara, Co. Longford.

23 **Lindsay Tribunal:** Former Health Minister Barry Desmond told the Lindsay tribunal he was appalled wrong information was given to him in the mid-1980s in relation to the viral inactivation of blood products used to treat haemophiliacs.

23 **Haughey:** Charles Haughey told the Moriarty tribunal he totally rejected claims that he diverted one penny from the funds raised to save the life of Brian Lenihan.

24 **Ansbacher:** A court in the Cayman Islands ruled that confidential information relating to the Ansbacher deposits should be passed to the Irish authorities, but not the identities of any of the depositors.

June

2 **Nice Treaty:** *Irish Times*/MRBI opinion poll showed significant movement from the yes to the no camp with 45 per cent intending to vote for the treaty (seven points down on the last poll) and 28 per cent intending to vote no (seven points higher than in the last poll).

5 **EU:** Charlie McCreevy, meeting his EU counterparts in Luxembourg, defied a call for action to offset the inflationary effect of last December's budget.

7 **Nice Treaty:** Irish voters' rejected the Treaty of Nice by 53.87 per cent to 46.13 per cent with a turnout of 35 per cent.

13 **Dual Mandate:** Plans by the Minister for the Environment, Noel Dempsey, to ban TDs from sitting on local authorities were been scrapped, following the threat by four Independent TDs to end their support for the government.

15 **Nice Treaty:** Charlie McCreevy last night described the Irish rejection of the Nice Treaty as a 'remarkably healthy development' and an anti-establishment statement of which the people should be proud. On 18 June Michael McDowell (Attorney General) addressing the Institute of European Affairs in a personal capacity said there was a sharp division between the federalist European project and what the Irish people wanted, and the people should not allow themselves to be silenced by a sense of gratitude or inhibited by a sense of relative size.

25 **Budget:** The Central Bank in its summer bulletin backed EU calls for a cautious budget this year. It warned that a giveaway pre-election budget would increase the risks of a hard landing for the Irish economy.

30 Voters in Tipperary South cast their by-election ballots in the first poll to be held in the Republic on a Saturday. Senator Tom Hayes (Fine Gael) was elected. The by-election was caused by the death of Theresa Ahern (Fine Gael) last year.

July

3 **Opinion Polls:** The Government decided to ban the publication of opinion polls during the last week of election campaigns.

5 **Opinion Polls:** The Attorney General warned that a ban on carrying out and publishing opinion polls in the seven days before a polling day could be unconstitutional.

8 **Election:** Speculation increased about an autumn general election when the Taoiseach suggested that TDs and senators who favour one should make their case to him. On 24 July the Taoiseach ruled out a general election before summer 2002, saying he had 'put it up to' colleagues to argue for an autumn 2001 poll, and none had done so.

11 **Opinion Polls:** The government was forced to drop the legislative amendment banning opinion polls in the last week of an election. The Tánaiste, Mary Harney, said that there had been a loophole in the bill which had come to light during examination in the Seanad (by Independent Senator Shane Ross) that would have allowed polls taken eight days before an election to be published on the day of an election, as well as exit polls to be taken and published that day.

12 **Jamie Sinnott:** The Supreme Court upheld an appeal by the state against a High Court ruling that it was obliged to provide education to Jamie Sinnott, a 23-year-old autistic

man, for as long as he could benefit from it. The state successfully argued that the High Court had breached the principle of the separation of powers between the judiciary and the Oireachtas by actually telling the government what education service to provide. Last October the High Court awarded Sinnott £225,000, and his mother Kathryn Sinnott £55,000. The state will pay the money awarded to Sinnott and his mother despite the Supreme Court ruling against them. On 16 July the Government confirmed that it would appeal the decision on legal costs in the Sinnott case. However, the Minister for Education, Michael Woods, said this did not mean that Kathryn Sinnott would end up having to pay any costs for the case.

17 **Abbeylara:** The High Court began hearing a challenge by gardaí to the inquiry by an Oireachtas subcommittee into the shooting dead of John Carthy.

25 **Nice Treaty:** Fine Gael announced that they would not participate in the National Forum on Europe that is intended to deal with the fallout from the Nice Treaty rejection.

27 **Lindsay Tribunal:** The Lindsay tribunal rejected an application by the Irish Haemophilia Society to investigate certain actions of pharmaceutical companies which supplied infected blood products to the state.

31 **Lawlor:** The High Court ruled that Liam Lawlor had again failed to co-operate fully with the Flood tribunal. On 3 August Lawlor avoided a return to prison after the Supreme Court granted a stay pending an appeal.

August

6 **Decommissioning:** Statement issued by the Independent International Commission on Decommissioning that the IRA had proposed a method to put its weapons beyond use.

8 **Decommissioning:** The Provisional IRA said that it had 'agreed' a scheme with the Independent International Commission on Decommissioning (IICD) which will put its weapons 'completely and verifiably beyond use'.

10 **Dual Mandate:** Minister for the Environment, Mr Dempsey, confirmed that the annual £10,000 salary-type payment paid to county councillors will be withheld from the 113 TDs and senators who are also county councillors.

September

3 Oireachtas inquiry into a £36 million overrun on a CIÉ rail signalling project began.

8 **Election:** The Taoiseach appears on RTÉ's soccer show 'The Premiership'.

11 The Taoiseach, Tánaiste and Opposition leaders condemned the attacks on the World Trade Center and Pentagon. The government set up 24-hour phone lines for concerned relatives of Irish people living in the US.

14 **Abortion:** New guidelines issued by the Medical Council. The Medical Council voted, by 14 votes to 8, to adopt a new guideline on abortion: the termination of a pregnancy was permissible where there was 'a real and substantial risk to the life of the mother'.

21 The government agreed to allow US forces engaged in a military response to the attacks in America to refuel at Irish airports and fly over Irish airspace.

23 Former Fianna Fáil minister Kevin Boland died aged 84.

28 **Abortion:** The Labour Party voted for the introduction of abortion on the basis of a woman's right to choose. The vote came at the party's conference in Cork and was against the wishes of the leadership.

October

1 **UN:** Ireland's presidency of the UN Security Council for the month of October began.

14 Eighty years after they were put to death the state celebrated the funerals of Kevin Barry and nine comrades.

18 **Nice Treaty:** The Government's National Forum on Europe was officially launched in Dublin Castle in the absence of Fine Gael.

19 The Chief Justice, Mr Justice Keane, ordered that Denis Riordan be prevented from taking legal proceedings in either the High or Supreme Courts against the Taoiseach, the government or the state without the Supreme Court's prior permission. He said that Riordan had not merely repeatedly sought to reopen decisions of the court but he had persistently abused his right to appear in court in cases in which he had no direct interest in order to make 'scandalous allegations, not merely against members of the judiciary but other persons whom he chose to join as defendants in his proceedings'. A week earlier Riordan was freed by the Supreme Court, having spent seven days in prison when he refused to withdraw remarks that the three judges hearing his applications were 'corrupt'.

22 **Haughey:** The High Court ruled that a taxing master, James Flynn, must withdraw from a hearing on costs incurred by the Haughey family during challenges to the Moriarty tribunal. Mr Justice Kelly handed the matter over to the other High Court taxing master, Charles Moran.

23 **Decommissioning:** It was announced that the IRA allowed Gen. de Chastelain and two of his colleagues to witness it putting some of its weapons beyond use.

25 **Abortion:** Debate in the Dáil on the government's proposal.

26 **Nice Treaty:** The first full session of the National Forum on Europe took place (without the participation of the Progressive Democrats, who claimed they were not notified of the event).

30 **Lowry:** Michael Lowry told the Moriarty tribunal he did not interfere at any level in the process of awarding a mobile phone licence to Esat Digifone in 1996.

November

4 **ASTI:** Survey finds that the membership was overwhelmingly opposed to further industrial action.

5 Fine Gael proposed legislation under which Travellers camped illegally on public or private ground would be forced to move on or face arrest.

7 Tourism Ireland, the first all-Ireland Tourism Marketing Programme set up under the Belfast Agreement, was launched in Dublin. It is to spend £60 million promoting Ireland as a safe and welcoming destination.

13 **Burke:** The Flood tribunal discovered three accounts of Ray Burke (two of them offshore) which the former minister had previously failed to disclose. He said the money came from the sale of his insurance business and fees earned on house sales.

22 The opposition boycotted the Dáil for a second day in protest over allegations of corruption made against a former Fine Gael Minister Nora Owen who said she had been 'ruined' by the untrue and unfounded allegations made by the independent Donegal deputy, Thomas Gildea, in the Dáil chamber on Wednesday night. During a debate on a Fine Gael private members' motion calling for a tribunal of inquiry into the McBrearty affair, Gildea said Owen should be investigated for abusing her powers and putting unacceptable pressure on gardaí in Donegal when in office. Gildea, withdrew his allegations after being requested to do so and apologised to Owen and her party 'for the hurt caused'.

23 **Abbeylara:** The High Court upheld a challenge by 36 members of the Garda Emergency Response Unit against the conduct of the inquiry into the killing of John Carthy in April 2000. The three judges found that Oireachtas inquiries cannot make 'findings of fact or expressions of opinion' which damage the good name of citizens who are not TDs or senators.

26 **Health Strategy:** The Minister for Health, Micheál Martin, launched the long-awaited Health Strategy.

26 **Lawlor:** Liam Lawlor's appeal against a further term of imprisonment on contempt charges began.

27 **Abbeylara:** The Attorney General to appeal the High Court's ruling limiting the scope of Oireachtas investigations to the Supreme Court.

30 **Abortion:** Cardinal Alfonso López Trujillo, an influential cardinal in the Vatican, is reported to have said he expects the Irish Catholic hierarchy to oppose the Government's abortion referendum legislation.

30 **Election:** Fine Gael and Labour agreed on joint actions in the Dáil, following official talks on maximising their impact in the run up to the general election.

December

1 The Government nominated High Court judge, Mr Justice Joseph Finnegan, as President of the Court to replace Mr Justice Frederick Morris.

5 **Budget Day**

9 **Election:** Pat Rabbitte and Róisín Shorthall, members of Labour's front bench, publicly stated their opposition to a coalition with Fianna Fáil.

10 **Election:** It was reported that at a Christmas party in the members' restaurant in Leinster House last week, Ruairí Quinn, in a rallying pre-election speech delivered shortly before 11pm, told guests, mainly Labour Party members, that the key task in the new year would be to 'get the bastards out'. Fianna Fáil took serious umbrage at the remarks. Rather than apologise, Labour went on the offensive with Eamon Gilmore saying he had no idea Fianna Fáil were such 'delicate flowers' and had led such sheltered lives that the use of a rude word had them all rushing for the smelling salts.

12 **Abortion:** The bishops welcomed the proposed referendum as it did not 'dilute or weaken the general protection already afforded the unborn by Article 40.3.3 of the Constitution'. As such, 'Catholic voters should feel free in conscience to support this measure, even if it is viewed as less than might have been desired'.

12 **Lawlor:** The Supreme Court upheld a decision to impose a seven-day prison sentence and £5,000 fine on Liam Lawlor.

12 **Referendum Commission:** Role of the Referendum Commission changed so that it will not be presenting both sides of the issue in future referendum campaigns. The commission will publish and distribute statements through television, radio and other electronic media 'which the commission considers most likely to bring them to the attention of the electorate'.

17 **EU:** European leaders launched a review of the European Union aimed at making the European institutions more effective and democratic. The Convention on the Future of Europe will meet from March next year with a broad mandate to examine the strengths and weaknesses of the EU. The Taoiseach acknowledged that the convention could put sensitive issues for Ireland, such as tax harmonisation, back on the table for debate. The convention will be chaired by the former French president, Mr Valéry Giscard d'Estaing, assisted by the former Italian Prime Minister, Mr Giuliano Amato and the former Belgian Prime Minister, Mr Jean Luc Dehaene.

17 **Abortion:** The Pro-Life Campaign said it will 'work enthusiastically' to encourage voters to support the Government's abortion referendum proposal early in the new year.

19 **ASTI:** The ASTI voted overwhelmingly to support non co-operation with in-service training and new Department of Education programmes.

28 **Election:** Fianna Fáil believed it could raise £2.5 million to enable it to spend the £2.7 million it is allowed in next year's general election campaign.

31 **Euro:** Last day before the introduction of the euro.

Source: Irish Times.

6. Bye-Election Results

TABLE 6.1

TIPPERARY SOUTH BYE-ELECTION, 30 JUNE 2001

Candidate	Party	First Count	Eliminate Landy	Second Count	Eliminate Maguire	Third Count
Hayes, Tom	Fine Gael	11,446 (35.9%)	1,067	12,513	3,278	15,791
Landy, Denis	Labour	4,103 (12.9%)	−4,103			
Maguire, Michael	Fianna Fáil	8,461 (26.5%)	790	9,251	−9,251	
Prendergast, Phil	Independent	7,897 (24.7%)	1,479	9,376	3,515	12,891
Non-transferable			767		2,458	

Electorate = 54,542, Total Valid Poll = 31,907, Quota = 15,954.

Source: Fine Gael Press Office.

7. Constituency Opinion Polls

TABLE 7.1

MAYO, JANUARY 2001

Candidate (First Preference)	Number of Respondents
Caffrey, Ernie (FG)	12
Carty, John (FF)	24
Chambers, Frank (FF)	21
Cooper-Flynn, Beverley (FF)	42
Crowley, Ann (GP)	4
Cullen, Cormack Connie (Ind)	
Finn, Richard (Ind)	14
Ginty, Gerry (Ind)	5
Higgins, Jim (FG)	56
Kenny, Enda (FG)	35
Kilcoyne, Michael (Lab)	2
Moffat, Tom (FF)	18
Ring, Michael (FG)	66
Sherry, Ciaran (Ind)	1
Woods, Vincent (SF)	4
Don't know	70
Will not vote	50
Refused	6
Total	430

Source: TG4/MRBI.

TABLE 7.2

TIPPERARY NORTH, FEBRUARY 2001

Candidate (First Preference)	Number of Respondents
Carey, Margaret (National Party)	6
Coonan, Noel (FG)	52
Hoctor, Maire (FF)	39
Lowry, Michael (Ind)	108
Mac Bain, Gillies (Ind)	–
O'Meara, Kathleen (Lab)	43
Smith, Michael (FF)	91
Don't know	32
Will not vote	28
Refused	1
Total	400

Sources: TG4/MRBI.

TABLE 7.3

TIPPERARY SOUTH, JUNE 2001

Candidate (First Preference)	Number of Respondents
Hayes, Tom (FG)	107
Landy, Denis (Lab)	52
Maguire, Michael (FF)	77
Predergast, Phil (Ind)	93
Don't know	44
Will not vote	18
Refused	8
Total	399

Sources: TG4/MRBI.

TABLE 7.4

KERRY NORTH, OCTOBER 2001

Candidate (First Preference)	Number of Respondents
Deenihan, Jimmy (FG)	76
Ferris, Martin (SF)	75
Kiely, Dan (FF)	37
McEllistrim, Tom (FF)	55
Spring, Dick (Lab)	78
Don't know	53
Will not vote	16
Refused	10
Total	400

Sources: TG4/MRBI.

TABLE 7.5

SLIGO-LEITRIM, DECEMBER 2001

Candidate (First Preference)	Number of Respondents
Bree, Declan (Lab)	19
Devins, Jimmy (FF)	32
Ellis, John (FF)	38
Harkin, Marian (Ind)	64
MacManus, Sean (SF)	26
Perry, John (FG)	73
Reynolds, Gerry (FG)	33
Scanlan, Eamon (FF)	25
Don't know	74
Will not vote	9
Refused	7
Total	400

Sources: TG4/MRBI.

TABLE 7.6

DUBLIN SOUTH WEST, DECEMBER 2001

Candidate (First Preference)	Number of Respondents
Crowe, Sean (SF)	55
Federsel, Monique (GP)	13
Hayes, Brian (FG)	72
Kinsella, Marie (Ind)	9
Lenihan, Conor (FF)	55
O'Connor, Charlie (FF)	25
Murphy, Mick (SP)	4
Rabbitte, Pat (Lab)	62
Walsh, Eamonn (Lab)	8
Don't know	56
Will not vote	29
Refused	15
Total	403

Source: TG4/MRBI.

8. Referendum Results

TABLE 8.1

DEATH PENALTY

(REFERENDUM ON TWENTY-FIRST AMENDMENT OF THE
CONSTITUTION (NO. 2) BILL, 2001)

Constituency	Electorate	Total Poll	Percentage Poll	Percentage in Favour	Percentage Against	Spoilt Votes
Carlow-Kilkenny	92,470	31,543	34.11	57.90	40.51	502
Cavan-Monaghan	85,803	29,758	34.68	61.76	36.24	597
Clare	76,227	23,500	30.83	61.52	36.93	364
Cork East	68,707	24,481	35.63	58.88	39.58	377
Cork North-Central	75,038	25,090	33.44	58.67	39.94	349
Cork North-West	49,749	18,632	37.45	58.36	39.52	394
Cork South-Central	90,790	33,742	37.16	62.82	36.06	379
Cork South-West	50,677	18,779	37.06	61.26	36.71	381
Donegal North-East	55,035	15,201	27.62	61.87	36.54	242
Donegal South-West	52,671	15,049	28.57	58.38	40.06	234
Dublin Central	61,290	20,631	33.66	60.27	38.27	300
Dublin North	70,321	26,577	37.79	64.38	34.79	222
Dublin North-Central	64,007	27,645	43.19	62.24	36.85	251
Dublin North-East	59,877	23,898	39.91	62.51	36.67	195
Dublin North-West	57,284	21,931	38.28	61.88	37.11	222
Dublin South	93,038	39,531	42.49	69.66	29.63	281
Dublin South-Central	65,542	25,624	39.10	62.79	35.85	347
Dublin South-East	58,820	23,304	39.62	71.07	27.44	348
Dublin South-West	81,266	25,900	31.87	56.99	42.02	255
Dublin West	77,760	26,762	34.42	62.49	36.87	171
Dun Laoghaire	86,549	37,056	42.82	71.31	27.95	276
Galway East	65,633	19,445	29.63	60.29	37.62	406
Galway West	83,176	24,561	29.53	64.82	33.53	406
Kerry North	53,366	17,486	32.77	56.30	42.09	281
Kerry South	48,992	15,701	32.05	60.74	37.49	278
Kildare North	59,035	20,329	34.44	64.08	34.86	216
Kildare South	51,142	16,517	32.30	57.88	40.75	226
Laoghis-Offaly	90,987	29,272	32.17	57.07	40.92	589
Limerick East	80,339	27,729	34.51	57.47	41.11	394
Limerick West	49,160	17,106	34.80	57.77	40.02	379
Longford-Roscommon	67,305	21,519	31.97	59.32	38.92	378
Louth	78,007	26,485	33.95	58.96	39.82	322
Mayo	90,336	27,195	30.10	58.51	39.48	546
Meath	101,888	33,210	32.59	60.89	37.89	407
Sligo-Leitrim	66,748	23,489	35.19	59.15	38.68	509
Tipperary North	56,278	19,115	33.97	60.63	37.37	382
Tipperary South	53,463	19,804	37.04	57.43	40.34	442
Waterford	71,946	25,158	34.97	59.56	38.85	399
Westmeath	51,664	16,321	31.59	57.50	40.79	279
Wexford	90,507	30,228	33.40	57.73	40.49	538
Wicklow	85,067	32,581	38.30	60.69	38.03	416
Total	2,867,960	997,885	34.79	61.17	37.37	14,480

Source: Irish Times.

33

TABLE 8.2

NICE TREATY

(REFERENDUM ON TWENTY-SECOND AMENDMENT OF THE
CONSTITUTION BILL, 2001)

Constituency	Electorate	Total Poll	Percentage Poll	Percentage in Favour	Percentage Against	Spoilt Votes
Carlow-Kilkenny	92,470	31,548	34.12	46.91	51.34	552
Cavan-Monaghan	85,803	29,712	34.63	47.22	50.97	536
Clare	76,227	23,504	30.83	47.93	50.43	386
Cork East	68,707	24,474	35.62	42.86	55.62	371
Cork North-Central	75,038	25,080	33.42	40.38	58.41	305
Cork North-West	49,749	18,646	37.48	44.11	53.51	444
Cork South-Central	90,790	33,740	37.16	45.73	53.21	360
Cork South-West	50,677	18,777	37.05	46.47	51.68	348
Donegal North-East	55,035	15,175	27.57	39.23	59.18	242
Donegal South-West	52,671	15,048	28.57	39.07	59.55	208
Dublin Central	61,290	20,634	33.67	39.33	59.11	322
Dublin North	70,321	26,584	37.80	47.53	51.52	254
Dublin North-Central	64,007	27,634	43.17	42.53	56.58	246
Dublin North-East	59,877	23,843	39.82	43.16	55.94	214
Dublin North-West	57,284	21,937	38.30	41.38	57.53	238
Dublin South	93,038	39,585	42.55	51.46	47.73	322
Dublin South-Central	65,542	25,618	39.09	43.72	55.20	278
Dublin South-East	58,820	23,321	39.65	48.57	49.95	344
Dublin South-West	81,266	25,902	31.87	38.05	60.99	249
Dublin West	77,760	26,746	34.40	43.77	55.54	182
Dun Laoghaire	86,549	37,046	42.80	53.05	45.97	362
Galway East	65,633	19,441	29.62	46.34	51.61	398
Galway West	83,176	24,571	29.54	41.11	56.78	520
Kerry North	53,366	17,491	32.78	38.80	59.61	279
Kerry South	48,992	15,684	32.01	44.15	54.11	274
Kildare North	59,035	20,336	34.45	48.80	50.14	217
Kildare South	51,142	16,515	32.29	47.05	51.55	231
Laoghis-Offaly	90,987	29,274	32.17	47.65	50.34	588
Limerick East	80,339	27,725	34.51	45.88	52.63	412
Limerick West	49,160	17,106	34.80	48.21	49.55	384
Longford-Roscommon	67,305	21,526	31.98	46.40	51.70	410
Louth	78,007	26,489	33.96	46.07	52.75	314
Mayo	90,336	27,195	30.10	43.39	54.66	531
Meath	101,888	33,209	32.59	47.31	51.21	492
Sligo-Leitrim	66,748	23,505	35.21	43.83	53.91	531
Tipperary North	56,278	19,105	33.95	48.47	49.58	373
Tipperary South	53,463	19,801	37.04	47.52	50.33	426
Waterford	71,946	25,159	34.97	47.37	50.86	445
Westmeath	51,664	16,322	31.59	44.31	54.00	275
Wexford	90,507	30,231	33.40	47.84	50.35	550
Wicklow	85,067	32,587	38.31	45.54	53.01	474
Total	2,867,960	997,826	34.79	45.44	53.06	14,887

Source: *Irish Times.*

TABLE 8.3

INTERNATIONAL CRIMINAL COURT
(REFERENDUM ON TWENTY-THIRD AMENDMENT OF THE
CONSTITUTION BILL, 2001)

Constituency	Electorate	Total Poll	Percentage Poll	Percentage in Favour	Percentage Against	Spoilt Votes
Carlow-Kilkenny	92,470	31,536	34.10	62.62	35.18	695
Cavan-Monaghan	85,803	29,698	34.61	63.31	34.29	711
Clare	76,227	23,504	30.83	64.89	33.05	486
Cork East	68,707	24,480	35.63	58.91	39.03	505
Cork North-Central	75,038	25,053	33.39	59.14	39.18	419
Cork North-West	49,749	18,627	37.44	58.46	38.69	531
Cork South-Central	90,790	33,739	37.16	65.54	33.03	483
Cork South-West	50,677	18,770	37.04	63.23	34.21	479
Donegal North-East	55,035	15,176	27.58	55.65	42.36	302
Donegal South-West	52,671	15,043	28.56	54.34	43.69	296
Dublin Central	61,290	20,636	33.67	55.13	43.25	333
Dublin North	70,321	26,560	37.77	68.76	30.27	259
Dublin North-Central	64,007	27,605	43.13	63.36	35.85	218
Dublin North-East	59,877	23,857	39.84	64.63	34.29	257
Dublin North-West	57,284	21,937	38.30	61.78	36.95	279
Dublin South	93,038	39,528	42.49	71.33	27.65	404
Dublin South-Central	65,542	25,624	39.10	62.79	35.85	347
Dublin South-East	58,820	23,310	39.63	67.68	30.31	467
Dublin South-West	81,266	25,892	31.86	60.30	38.61	283
Dublin West	77,760	26,780	34.44	67.05	32.12	223
Dun Laoghaire	86,549	37,014	42.77	71.44	27.46	407
Galway East	65,633	19,443	29.62	61.84	35.75	469
Galway West	83,176	24,563	29.53	63.25	34.62	524
Kerry North	53,366	17,480	32.75	56.65	41.06	400
Kerry South	48,992	15,683	32.01	61.12	36.28	408
Kildare North	59,035	20,332	34.44	69.34	29.44	248
Kildare South	51,142	16,512	32.29	64.74	33.65	266
Laoghis-Offaly	90,987	29,274	32.17	62.24	35.45	675
Limerick East	80,339	27,718	34.50	62.35	36.13	423
Limerick West	49,160	17,097	34.78	60.98	36.13	493
Longford-Roscommon	67,305	21,521	31.98	60.19	37.56	484
Louth	78,007	26,481	33.95	62.04	36.51	386
Mayo	90,336	27,191	30.10	58.25	39.33	657
Meath	101,888	33,206	32.59	65.70	32.77	509
Sligo-Leitrim	66,748	23,498	35.20	59.58	38.00	568
Tipperary North	56,278	19,114	33.96	63.11	34.45	467
Tipperary South	53,463	19,807	37.05	61.08	36.38	504
Waterford	71,946	25,159	34.97	62.98	34.97	517
Westmeath	51,664	16,315	31.58	58.46	39.68	303
Wexford	90,507	30,230	33.40	63.37	34.62	607
Wicklow	85,067	32,572	38.29	64.56	33.82	527
Total	2,867,960	997,565	34.78	63.08	35.14	17,819

Source: Irish Times.

9. Opinion Polls

All figures are percentages. For details on the number of respondents see Table 9.50.

Party Support

TABLE 9.1
PARTY VOTE

'If there was a General Election tomorrow to which party or independent candidate would you give your first preference vote?' [All Expressing a Preference]

Date of Poll[a]	Fianna Fail			Fine Gael			Labour			Prog Dems			Green Party			Sinn Féin		
	J	M1	M2	J	M1	M2	J	M1	M2	J	M1	M2	J	M1	M2	J	M1	M2
Total	46	48	48	18	22	22	12	10	9	8	4	2	6	3	4	5	6	5
Sex																		
Male	43	47	47	16	19	23	14	11	10	3	2	2	4	3	3	8	9	6
Female	49	48	49	21	24	21	11	10	8	5	5	3	5	3	6	3	4	3
Age																		
18–24	42	41	48	16	22	17	10	9	10	4	3	1	7	4	10	15	9	7
25–34	47	47	48	17	21	18	13	12	9	4	4	1	5	7	6	7	6	10
35–49	45	44	50	17	21	18	14	13	9	2	–	3	5	3	4	3	9	4
50–64	45	56	47	20	18	30	14	11	6	6	6	3	3	1	2	5	3	3
65+	53	53	47	23	27	30	10	4	13	4	6	3	3	1	1	3	3	1
Social Class																		
ABC1	47	46	45	21	24	20	10	11	12	5	3	3	5	4	8	3	5	4
C2DE	44	48	50	13	18	20	16	11	9	3	4	2	5	2	3	8	8	7
F	50	53	49	33	30	38	5	7	2	1	2	1	2	1	–	4	2	2
Geographical																		
Dublin	41	40	39	13	17	13	16	10	15	8	4	5	6	6	8	5	11	8
Rest of Leinster	50	51	52	17	19	28	10	14	8	3	3	2	7	3	4	6	3	2
Munster	44	51	55	23	23	22	13	10	6	2	4	1	2	1	4	4	4	3
Conn/Ulster	53	49	47	20	28	29	8	7	5	1	3	1	2	2	1	10	6	8
Urban/Rural																		
Urban	42	45	46	14	18	15	14	11	14	6	5	3	6	4	7	7	8	6
Rural	52	52	51	25	27	32	10	9	3	1	1	1	2	1	1	4	4	4

[a]Dates of Opinion Poll fieldwork: J: 22–3 January, M1: 14–15 May; and M2: 29–30 May.

Source: MRBI.

TABLE 9.2
PARTY VOTE

'If there were to be a General Election tomorrow, to which party would you give your first preference vote? To which party would you be most inclined to give your preference vote?' (Preference and Inclination) [Committed Voters]

Date of Poll[a]	Fianna Fail					Fine Gael					Labour					Prog Dems					Green Party					Sinn Féin				
	A	B	C	D	E	A	B	C	D	E	A	B	C	D	E	A	B	C	D	E	A	B	C	D	E	A	B	C	D	E
Total	46	51	49	51	54	25	13	24	22	19	11	14	13	10	11	4	3	3	3	4	4	4	5	4	4	4	9	4	6	5
Sex																														
Male	47	46	48	50	52	23	12	23	23	18	11	17	14	11	12	4	3	2	3	3	3	3	4	3	4	6	12	5	8	7
Female	45	55	50	53	55	26	14	24	22	20	12	12	12	10	9	3	3	3	3	5	6	6	5	5	3	2	6	3	3	3
Age																														
18–24	39	44	43	42	53	22	20	23	20	18	13	14	13	10	7	2	1	2	3	2	7	4	8	13	8	13	14	7	10	10
25–34	48	49	47	54	53	17	12	24	15	11	15	14	9	10	14	4	3	1	4	6	7	9	9	4	5	2	9	6	9	6
35–49	43	47	48	50	51	28	11	19	23	18	12	15	18	10	10	5	3	4	3	4	4	4	4	4	3	3	11	3	4	7
50–64	47	57	53	48	56	25	10	27	28	21	8	18	10	14	11	3	2	2	3	3	3	2	3	1	3	4	6	2	3	1
65+	56	63	53	62	56	30	18	29	25	28	8	9	11	7	10	4	4	3	1	2	1	*	*	*	1	1	4	3	3	2
Social Class																														
ABC1	42	51	48	54	51	26	16	21	21	19	10	15	10	8	9	6	3	3	5	6	7	6	10	6	5	4	6	4	3	5
C2DE	48	51	49	51	54	19	11	22	17	14	15	14	16	13	15	3	2	3	3	3	4	3	2	3	3	5	12	4	8	6
F	48	–	52	43	56	40	–	35	43	33	4	–	7	7	3	1	–	*	1	2	1	–	1	2	2	1	–	3	2	1
Geographical																														
Dublin	40	44	46	49	50	18	13	16	11	13	16	15	16	14	12	5	2	4	6	9	7	7	8	7	4	8	13	5	8	9
Rest of Leinster	51	58	54	53	57	23	14	19	20	19	12	13	16	15	12	2	1	1	3	2	6	3	5	3	3	4	8	4	4	7
Munster	45	54	46	48	51	27	16	30	31	22	12	18	12	8	13	4	3	3	2	2	3	2	3	3	3	2	4	3	3	1
Conn/Ulster	49	71	51	58	59	31	11	32	27	23	3	3	4	3	4	4	5	2	1	2	2	–	2	3	4	2	5	4	7	2
Urban/Rural																														
Urban[b]	45	44	46	51	51	19	13	20	17	14	14	15	16	12	13	5	2	4	4	6	6	7	7	5	4	6	13	5	6	7
Rural[c]	46	58	52	51	57	32	14	28	29	25	8	14	10	8	7	2	3	2	2	1	2	2	2	3	3	2	5	3	5	2

[a]Dates of opinion poll fieldwork: (A) 1 Feb. 2001, (B) 8 Mar. 2001, (C) 17 May 2001, (D) 27 Sept. 2001, (E) 18 Dec. 2001; [b]For poll B: urban refers to Dublin; [c]For poll B: rural refers to areas other than Dublin.

Source: IMS.

37

Government Satisfaction

TABLE 9.3

GOVERNMENT SATISFACTION

'Would you say you are satisfied or dissatisfied with the manner in which the Government is running the country' [all respondents]

	Satisfied			Dissatisfied		
Date of Poll[a]	Jan	May1	May2	Jan	May1	May2
Total	58	59	62	35	33	32
Sex						
Male	64	61	67	32	33	28
Female	51	57	56	38	34	36
Age						
18–24	55	54	62	31	29	28
25–34	60	58	59	31	33	33
35–49	55	58	62	39	37	33
50–64	59	60	62	38	34	34
65+	60	66	65	34	30	30
Social Class						
ABC1	62	61	64	34	32	30
C2DE	53	55	59	38	37	35
F	62	73	66	27	22	27
Geographical						
Dublin	53	47	57	40	45	38
Rest of Leinster	52	63	62	37	28	31
Munster	62	64	65	34	28	29
Conn/Ulster	66	66	65	26	31	28
Urban/Rural						
Urban	54	55	60	40	39	35
Rural	62	65	64	29	25	27
Party						
FF	81	82	87	14	15	10
FG	42	51	44	48	40	45
Labour	43	51	54	53	47	45
PD	53	55	70	47	41	25
Other	48	33	48	47	58	48
DK	39	42	37	47	41	50

[a]Dates of opinion poll fieldwork: Jan: 22–3 January, May1: 14–15 May; and May2: 29–30 May.

Source: MRBI.

TABLE 9.4

GOVERNMENT SATISFACTION

Are you satisfied or dissatisfied with the may the Government is running the country?

	Satisfied					Dissatisfied				
Date of Poll[a]	A	B	C	D	E	A	B	C	D	E
Total	60	55	61	64	60	34	38	33	28	34
Sex										
Male	64	54	59	67	59	32	39	35	29	37
Female	57	57	62	62	61	35	38	31	28	31
Age										
18–24	57	53	59		60	33	34	31		30
25–34	62	56	62	60	62	31	38	31	30	31
35–49	57	55	59	67	60	36	40	36	27	34
50–64	59	60	59	61	54	36	328	36	33	43
65+	71	50	67	73	66	28	46	30	24	30
Social Class										
ABC1	62	58	57	66	62	33	35	37	25	34
C2DE	59	53	63		57	33	41	31		35
F	60	–	61	69	64	35	–	33	25	31
Geographical										
Dublin	53	52	56	57	56	41	43	36	37	37
Rest of Leinster	60	58	61	73	59	33	29	34	21	35
Munster	63	57	62	62	60	31	39	32	27	35
Conn/Ulster	69	70	66	69	69	28	27	28	26	25
Urban/Rural										
Urban[b]	58	52	58	63	57	35	43	36	30	38
Rural[c]	63	60	65	67	64	31	34	30	26	28
Party										
FF	82	82	86	87	83	15	15	11	10	14
FG	43	35	39	51	34	51	60	58	40	58
Labour	58	37	48	49	31	36	54	44	47	64
PD	67	58	79	56	84	27	33	21	30	16
Green Party	40	20	37	40	36	58	80	56	51	51
Sinn Féin	35	28	47	39	29	62	65	50	53	67
Other	59	21	41	46	66	36	74	45	42	34
DK	50	52	51	57	52	34	38	39	32	34

[a]Dates of opinion poll fieldwork: (A) 1 Feb. 2001, (B) 8 Mar. 2001, (C) 17 May 2001, (D) 27 Sept. 2001, (E) 18 Dec. 2001; [b]for poll B: urban refers to Dublin; [c]for poll B: rural refers to areas other than Dublin.

Source: IMS.

Party Leaders

TABLE 9.5

SATISFACTION WITH TAOISEACH

	Satisfied		Dissatisfied	
	'Would you say you are satisfied or dissatisfied with the way Mr Ahern is doing his job as Taoiseach?' [all respondents]			
Date of Poll[a]	Jan	May1	Jan	May1
Total	66	64	27	28
Sex				
Male	66	65	28	28
Female	65	63	26	27
Age				
18–24	62	59	24	23
25–34	67	64	26	23
35–49	67	63	27	32
50–64	61	71	34	26
65+	71	64	23	34
Social Class				
ABC1	64	65	31	27
C2DE	63	63	27	29
F	79	69	17	26
Geographical				
Dublin	54	53	37	37
Rest of Leinster	66	68	25	23
Munster	71	71	24	24
Conn/Ulster	76	69	18	26
Urban/Rural				
Urban	61	61	31	31
Rural	71	68	22	24
Party				
FF	91	88	6	8
FG	51	49	44	45
Labour	48	59	46	32
PD	53	48	47	48
Other	50	38	42	51
DK	51	51	31	30

[a]Dates of opinion poll fieldwork: Jan: 22–3 January; and May1: 14–15 May.

Source: MRBI.

40

TABLE 9.6
SATISFACTION WITH TANAISTE

'Would you say you are satisfied or dissatisfied with the way Ms Harney is doing her job as Tanaiste?' [all respondents]

Date of Poll[a]	Satisfied		Dissatisfied	
	Jan	May1	Jan	May1
Total	54	59	34	27
Sex				
Male	48	57	40	29
Female	59	61	28	25
Age				
18–24	49	48	29	25
25–34	53	54	33	25
35–49	52	54	38	35
50–64	55	68	36	26
65+	60	76	27	18
Social Class				
ABC1	58	59	32	26
C2DE	47	58	37	29
F	66	64	25	23
Geographical				
Dublin	44	48	42	37
Rest of Leinster	54	58	34	25
Munster	58	68	33	20
Conn/Ulster	64	65	20	24
Urban/Rural				
Urban	49	57	38	29
Rural	60	62	27	23
Party				
FF	69	71	21	20
FG	51	61	38	28
Labour	38	59	51	31
PD	94	90	6	3
Other	33	40	51	41
DK	43	42	37	34

[a]Dates of opinion poll fieldwork: Jan: 22–3 January; and May1: 14–15 May.

Source: MRBI.

TABLE 9.7

SATISFACTION WITH TAOISEACH

Are you satisfied or dissatisfied with Mr Bertie Ahern as Taoiseach?

	Satisfied					Dissatisfied				
Date of Poll[a]	A	B	C	D	E	A	B	C	D	E
Total	68	63	65	70	69	26	31	28	24	25
Sex										
Male	71	62	64	68	67	25	32	31	27	29
Female	66	63	67	72	71	27	30	25	21	21
Age										
18–24	71	62	67	68	66	20	23	18	19	19
25–34	69	61	63	69	72	24	35	31	24	24
35–49	67	63	67	70	72	27	31	29	25	24
50–64	65	68	64	67	67	32	31	32	29	29
65+	70	60	66	78	67	27	36	30	20	28
Social Class										
ABC1	71	65	64	71	69	24	29	29	22	27
C2DE	67	61	66	68	70	27	33	26	25	23
F	68	–	65	73	68	28	–	32	23	26
Geographical										
Dublin	66	61	61	66	68	27	32	29	27	26
Rest of Leinster	71	72	73	79	70	25	20	24	16	24
Munster	63	60	59	64	65	30	37	35	30	30
Conn/Ulster	76	68	73	75	76	20	25	22	20	17
Urban/Rural										
Urban[b]	67	61	63	67	67	27	32	29	27	28
Rural[c]	70	65	68	74	72	24	29	27	20	21
Party										
FF	89	89	90	90	90	8	8	8	7	7
FG	48	35	40	56	45	48	57	56	40	50
Labour	66	46	59	52	44	31	51	36	43	52
PD	82	58	63	56	85	18	25	21	26	15
Green Party	45	35	42	51	43	48	65	49	43	41
Sinn Féin	54	42	59	55	46	46	53	35	41	45
Other	68	32	55	58	72	25	58	32	38	28
DK	58	61	60	63	64	28	29	28	23	24

[a]Dates of opinion poll fieldwork: (A) 1 Feb. 2001, (B) 8 Mar. 2001, (C) 17 May 2001, (D) 27 Sept, 2001, (E) 18 Dec. 2001; [b]for poll B: urban refers to Dublin; [c]for poll B: rural refers to areas other than Dublin.

Source: IMS.

TABLE 9.8

SATISFACTION WITH PROGRESSIVE DEMOCRAT LEADER

'Are you satisfied or dissatisfied with the way Mary Harney is doing her job as leader of the Progressive Democrats?'

Date of Poll[a]	Satisfied					Dissatisfied				
	A	B	C	D	E	A	B	C	D	E
Total	59	56	59	59	58	31	31	30	30	30
Sex										
Male	54	51	55	52	54	38	37	32	37	36
Female	65	60	62	65	62	24	27	27	23	24
Age										
18–24	59	53	54	50	48	24	25	20	27	25
25–34	57	50	56	61	53	33	37	30	27	32
35–49	59	54	58	61	60	32	35	33	31	32
50–64	57	59	63	58	62	39	34	33	33	33
65+	66	72	65	61	67	24	19	30	32	25
Social Class										
ABC1	62	58	57	59	60	28	30	31	30	28
C2DE	58	54	59	57	54	31	33	28	31	31
F	58	–	62	64	65	35	–	31	26	30
Geographical										
Dublin	52	51	58	56	53	38	35	28	34	34
Rest of Leinster	62	50	63	64	56	30	32	29	24	31
Munster	62	65	55	52	59	27	28	33	35	30
Conn/Ulster	63	75	60	66	68	28	16	29	25	20
Urban/Rural										
Urban[b]	59	51	59	55	55	32	35	29	34	32
Rural[c]	60	61	59	63	63	30	28	31	25	26
Party										
FF	68	74	72	70	70	23	17	20	23	23
FG	55	57	46	55	57	39	33	45	38	37
Labour	46	47	50	55	43	48	46	36	40	46
PD	82	67	88	93	91	18	17	13	7	6
Green Party	53	25	47	31	48	28	65	44	49	40
Sinn Féin	32	26	65	49	33	59	63	26	43	61
Other	68	32	45	54	67	25	47	32	29	30
DK	57	51	53	47	39	27	25	27	31	28

[a]Dates of opinion poll fieldwork: (A) 1 Feb. 2001, (B) 8 Mar. 2001, (C) 17 May 2001, (D) 27 Sept. 2001, (E) 18 Dec. 2001; [b]for poll B: urban refers to Dublin; [c]for poll B: rural refers to areas other than Dublin.

Source: IMS.

TABLE 9.9

SATISFACTION WITH FINE GAEL LEADER

Bruton (Jan. only): 'Would you say you are satisfied or dissatisfied with the way Mr Bruton is doing his job as leader of Fine Gael?' [all respondents]; Noonan (May1 only): 'Would you say you are satisfied or dissatisfied with the way Mr Noonan is doing his job as leader of Fine Gael?' [all respondents]

Date of Poll[a]	Satisfied		Dissatisfied	
	Jan	May1	Jan	May1
Total	37	37	43	28
Sex				
Male	33	36	49	33
Female	41	38	36	23
Age				
18–24	33	27	30	20
25–34	37	32	37	20
35–49	33	36	47	34
50–64	39	39	53	33
65+	47	51	41	29
Social Class				
ABC1	35	39	46	27
C2DE	36	32	41	29
F	49	50	38	24
Geographical				
Dublin	29	28	49	31
Rest of Leinster	34	34	44	26
Munster	46	44	37	22
Conn/Ulster	41	43	39	33
Urban/Rural				
Urban	33	32	45	31
Rural	43	44	39	24
Party				
FF	35	32	46	31
FG	72	63	23	14
Labour	34	41	45	26
PD	31	34	59	34
Other	23	23	50	41
DK	27	30	40	22

[a]Dates of opinion poll fieldwork: Jan: 22–3 January; and May1: 14–15 May.

Source: MRBI.

TABLE 9.10

SATISFACTION WITH LABOUR LEADER

	Satisfied		Dissatisfied	
	'Would you say you are satisfied or dissatisfied with the way Mr Quinn is doing his job as leader of the Labour Party?' [all respondents]			
Date of Poll[a]	Jan	May1	Jan	May1
Total	48	47	29	24
Sex				
Male	50	49	29	28
Female	46	44	22	20
Age				
18–24	39	32	23	16
25–34	47	45	22	18
35–49	54	44	23	29
50–64	45	52	35	27
65+	50	60	26	24
Social Class				
ABC1	47	47	26	23
C2DE	48	44	25	25
F	48	56	25	20
Geographical				
Dublin	45	40	29	32
Rest of Leinster	43	50	26	18
Munster	52	50	23	20
Conn/Ulster	53	47	23	24
Urban/Rural				
Urban	47	44	26	27
Rural	49	50	25	19
Party				
FF	46	43	28	27
FG	60	61	19	13
Labour	68	67	18	15
PD	44	52	28	31
Other	46	34	35	36
DK	33	38	22	21

[a]Dates of opinion poll fieldwork: Jan: 22–3 January; and May1: 14–15 May.

Source: MRBI.

TABLE 9.11

SATISFACTION WITH FINE GAEL LEADER

Bruton: 'Were you satisfied or dissatisfied with the way Mr John Bruton did his job as leader of Fine Gael?' [A Only]; Noonan: 'Are you satisfied or dissatisfied with the way Mr Michael Noonan is doing his job as leader of Fine Gael?' [B–E Only]

	Satisfied					Dissatisfied				
Date of Poll[a]	A	B	C	D	E	A	B	C	D	E
Total	44	32	40	41	32	36	29	27	26	38
Sex										
Male	43	31	41	41	32	41	31	30	29	44
Female	46	33	39	42	32	31	27	25	23	33
Age										
18–24	38	32	35	34	25	31	16	17	19	25
25–34	31	35	39	39	31	39	31	28	27	35
35–49	42	31	36	42	32	41	31	34	25	43
50–64	55	33	46	41	35	32	35	26	29	46
65+	60	28	50	52	36	31	35	29	29	39
Social Class										
ABC1	41	31	38	39	32	41	27	31	28	41
C2DE	43	32	39	38	28	34	30	24	26	38
F	55	–	48	56	42	32	–	33	19	35
Geographical										
Dublin	39	26	29	28	25	39	31	29	29	38
Rest of Leinster	51	29	46	46	31	34	27	30	24	39
Munster	41	44	45	48	35	35	28	23	25	38
Conn/Ulster	50	43	44	44	38	34	27	29	25	37
Urban/Rural										
Urban[b]	39	26	35	36	29	39	31	27	29	39
Rural[c]	52	39	47	48	36	32	28	28	22	38
Party										
FF	45	36	35	39	31	36	29	31	28	42
FG	61	51	70	71	63	34	16	19	14	22
Labour	39	35	38	37	25	42	22	32	35	53
PD	36	33	38	26	36	52	17	29	37	36
Green Party	38	40	19	29	16	40	45	30	29	48
Sinn Féin	27	16	21	31	9	49	49	47	41	58
Other	41	32	32	25	22	43	37	36	54	45
DK	39	24	35	30	20	25	23	19	17	28

[a]Dates of opinion poll fieldwork: (A) 1 Feb. 2001, (B) 8 Mar. 2001, (C) 17 May 2001, (D) 27 Sept. 2001, (E) 18 Dec. 2001; [b]for poll B: urban refers to Dublin; [c]for poll B: rural refers to areas other than Dublin.

Source: IMS.

TABLE 9.12

SATISFACTION WITH LABOUR LEADER

'Are you satisfied or dissatisfied with the way Mr Ruairi Quinn is doing his job as leader of Labour?'

Date of Poll[a]	Satisfied					Dissatisfied				
	A	B	C	D	E	A	B	C	D	E
Total	53	52	52	47	40	21	23	21	24	35
Sex										
Male	55	52	52	48	43	25	25	24	27	39
Female	51	52	52	46	37	17	22	17	22	31
Age										
18–24	39	48	38	42	28	15	13	13	17	23
25–34	53	55	55	47	44	19	23	20	22	32
35–49	56	49	55	50	40	22	24	22	23	37
50–64	57	60	57	49	43	24	26	22	27	39
65+	56	47	52	46	43	25	36	26	35	42
Social Class										
ABC1	55	54	53	48	42	20	20	19	24	35
C2DE	50	50	51	46	39	23	26	19	25	34
F	57	–	53	49	40	15	–	29	22	40
Geographical										
Dublin	47	49	50	47	37	25	23	19	25	38
Rest of Leinster	51	47	56	48	35	22	23	20	20	37
Munster	55	59	52	49	48	18	24	21	27	28
Conn/Ulster	60	57	48	44	38	17	25	24	24	39
Urban/Rural										
Urban[b]	50	49	50	46	41	23	23	18	27	35
Rural[c]	56	55	54	49	38	19	24	24	21	36
Party										
FF	52	60	51	48	34	22	18	21	26	41
FG	66	60	57	56	52	17	14	24	25	32
Labour	72	75	81	75	74	18	18	11	13	16
PD	48	58	42	41	55	33	8	21	30	21
Green Party	40	40	44	49	36	23	45	19	20	35
Sinn Féin	30	35	50	35	23	32	37	32	41	60
Other	61	47	41	46	46	16	37	27	42	45
DK	37	36	40	35	30	18	21	15	17	25

[a]Dates of opinion poll fieldwork: (A) 1 Feb. 2001, (B) 8 Mar. 2001, (C) 17 May 2001, (D) 27 Sept. 2001, (E) 18 Dec. 2001; [b]for poll B: urban refers to Dublin; [c]for poll B: rural refers to areas other than Dublin.

Source: IMS.

Economy

TABLE 9.13

BUDGET 1

	'Do you think that your standard of living will rise, fall or remain the same as a result of the budget in December?' [22–3 May]		
	Rise	Same	Fall
Total	35	51	11
Sex			
Male	38	47	12
Female	31	56	10
Age			
18–24	31	53	10
25–34	37	51	10
35–49	32	54	13
50–64	36	50	10
65+	38	47	12
Social Class			
ABC1	36	52	9
C2DE	32	51	13
F	38	49	9
Geographical			
Dublin	32	51	14
Rest of Leinster	35	49	11
Munster	32	55	12
Conn/Ulster	44	47	4
Urban/Rural			
Urban	33	52	12
Rural	37	50	10
Party			
FF	42	49	5
FG	38	50	11
Labour	27	51	21
PD	38	53	9
Other	27	52	17
DK	25	57	14

Source: MRBI.

TABLE 9.14

BUDGET 2

	'In your opinion, was this budget good for the country or bad for the country?' [22–3 May]	
	Good	Bad
Total	71	15
Sex		
Male	73	15
Female	69	14
Age		
18–24	69	9
25–34	73	16
35–49	70	18
50–64	72	16
65+	73	12
Social Class		
ABC1	70	17
C2DE	71	15
F	78	8
Geographical		
Dublin	64	18
Rest of Leinster	70	15
Munster	74	16
Conn/Ulster	82	7
Urban/Rural		
Urban	70	16
Rural	74	13
Party		
FF	85	8
FG	67	17
Labour	62	24
PD	78	13
Other	59	22
DK	60	16

Source: MRBI.

49

TABLE 9.15

TAX CUTS

	'The Government is promising more tax cuts in the next budget. Would you or would you not be prepared to sacrifice further tax cuts for a better health service?' [29–30 May]	
	Yes	No
Total	74	20
Sex		
Male	73	22
Female	76	18
Age		
18–24	71	22
25–34	75	20
35–49	76	22
50–64	77	15
65+	70	21
Social Class		
ABC1	78	18
C2DE	73	21
F	68	22
Geographical		
Dublin	73	23
Rest of Leinster	79	17
Munster	69	22
Conn/Ulster	77	16
Urban/Rural		
Urban	76	20
Rural	72	21
Party		
FF	76	19
FG	74	21
Labour	68	20
PD	70	25
Other	79	18
DK	69	22

Source: MRBI.

TABLE 9.16
GROWTH

| | 'Do you, or do you not, feel confident that the economic growth which Ireland has enjoyed over the last number of years is set to continue?' [29–30 May] | |
	Yes	No
Total	50	46
Sex		
Male	56	41
Female	44	50
Age		
18–24	51	44
25–34	45	51
35–49	48	47
50–64	55	43
65+	54	39
Social Class		
ABC1	54	43
C2DE	48	46
F	48	51
Geographical		
Dublin	42	55
Rest of Leinster	54	40
Munster	51	43
Conn/Ulster	56	42
Urban/Rural		
Urban	47	49
Rural	55	41
Party		
FF	57	40
FG	54	41
Labour	49	46
PD	40	60
Other	37	60
DK	44	48

Source: MRBI.

TABLE 9.17

SOCIAL PARTNERSHIP 1

	'There has been some discussion about the role that social partnership between Government, employers, unions, farmers and voluntary organisations has played a part in our prosperity. In your view, should social partnership continue, or not?' [29–30 May]	
	Yes	No
Total	72	13
Sex		
Male	76	14
Female	68	11
Age		
18–24	64	10
25–34	68	16
35–49	76	12
50–64	79	12
65+	69	11
Social Class		
ABC1	76	11
C2DE	69	13
F	72	12
Geographical		
Dublin	72	14
Rest of Leinster	74	12
Munster	73	11
Conn/Ulster	66	13
Urban/Rural		
Urban	72	14
Rural	72	11
Party		
FF	79	9
FG	75	14
Labour	74	9
PD	95	5
Other	61	25
DK	58	11

Source: MRBI.

TABLE 9.18

SOCIAL PARTNERSHIP 2

	'And has social partnership, or has it not, succeeded in making this a fairer society?' [29–30 May]	
	Yes	No
Total	62	20
Sex		
Male	65	22
Female	59	17
Age		
18–24	58	14
25–34	57	22
35–49	63	24
50–64	68	20
65+	65	14
Social Class		
ABC1	65	20
C2DE	59	21
F	64	15
Geographical		
Dublin	55	27
Rest of Leinster	70	14
Munster	65	19
Conn/Ulster	58	17
Urban/Rural		
Urban	58	24
Rural	68	13
Party		
FF	71	14
FG	68	18
Labour	61	21
PD	85	15
Other	48	34
DK	46	21

Source: MRBI.

TABLE 9.19

ECONOMIC DOWNTURN

'Following strong growth in recent years, the economy has now suffered a slow down. How long do you think the current downturn will continue for?' [18 December]

	< 1 Year	1 Year	2 Years	3–4 Years	5 Years or Longer
Total	8	21	29	15	8
Sex					
Male	11	19	31	15	8
Female	5	23	28	15	8
Age					
18–24	8	22	32	14	6
25–34	8	22	34	14	7
35–49	8	25	31	15	8
50–64	10	18	26	16	11
65+	6	16	21	17	9
Social Class					
ABC1	9	23	36	12	8
C2DE	8	19	25	17	9
F	6	22	27	16	7
Geographical					
Dublin	11	24	30	16	9
Rest of Leinster	9	20	31	15	8
Munster	4	15	29	17	9
Conn/Ulster	9	27	25	12	8
Urban/Rural					
Urban	8	21	31	17	9
Rural	8	21	27	13	8
Party					
FF	10	23	29	12	7
FG	7	20	27	18	11
Labour	10	22	34	10	7
PD	*	16	31	41	3
Green Party	4	19	29	29	*
Sinn Féin	11	20	31	20	9
Other	2	14	44	10	5
DK	5	21	25	16	8

Source: IMS.

TABLE 9.20

STANDARD OF LIVING

	Standard of Living: 'Taking everything into consideration would you say that your standard of living has improved, disimproved or remained the same over the past 12 months?' [18 December]		
	Improved	Disimproved	Same
Total	35	12	51
Sex			
Male	36	12	50
Female	35	12	52
Age			
18–24	42	8	48
25–34	41	11	45
35–49	36	13	50
50–64	30	15	52
65+	26	9	62
Social Class			
ABC1	39	12	48
C2DE	36	12	50
F	25	13	60
Geographical			
Dublin	45	12	40
Rest of Leinster	34	12	52
Munster	31	11	56
Conn/Ulster	27	14	59
Urban/Rural			
Urban	38	13	47
Rural	31	9	57
Party			
FF	39	8	50
FG	35	13	50
Labour	30	14	54
PD	57	12	31
Green Party	35	3	62
Sinn Féin	35	18	47
Other	27	17	51
DK	32	11	56

Source: IMS.

Health Services

TABLE 9.21

HEALTH SERVICES

	'Are you satisfied or dissatisfied with the state of the Health Service in this country?' [17 May]	
	Satisfied	Dissatisfied
Total	20	77
Sex		
Male	23	73
Female	17	80
Age		
18–24	25	67
25–34	24	70
35–49	12	87
50–64	20	79
65+	25	74
Social Class		
ABC1	18	79
C2DE	20	76
F	25	73
Geographical		
Dublin	14	82
Rest of Leinster	19	80
Munster	21	75
Conn/Ulster	30	66
Urban/Rural		
Urban	17	79
Rural	24	73
Party		
FF	23	75
FG	16	82
Labour	14	82
PD	25	75
Green Party	9	84
Sinn Féin	24	76
Other	23	77
DK	21	72

Source: IMS.

TABLE 9.22

BLAME FOR DEFICIENCIES

'Who do you think is most to blame for deficiencies in the Health Service: the current Government, successive governments or different occupational groups within the health service?' [17 May]

	Current Government	Successive Governments	Occupational Groups
Total	21	45	23
Sex			
Male	23	44	23
Female	20	46	23
Age			
18–24	23	31	27
25–34	24	44	19
35–49	18	52	26
50–64	19	49	23
65+	25	44	17
Social Class			
ABC1	21	48	23
C2DE	21	44	22
F	24	42	26
Geographical			
Dublin	23	49	19
Rest of Leinster	23	51	18
Munster	21	38	25
Conn/Ulster	18	41	34
Urban/Rural			
Urban	21	47	22
Rural	23	42	24
Party			
FF	17	48	26
FG	28	42	24
Labour	27	45	17
PD	29	42	25
Green Party	16	56	12
Sinn Féin	26	50	21
Other	18	50	32
DK	21	40	23

Source: IMS.

Abortion

TABLE 9.23

ABORTION

'The subject of abortion is being debated again, with the likelihood of a referendum at some stage in 2002. In what circumstances, if any, do you yourself believe that legal abortion should be available to Irish women? (A) No circumstances; (B) Where the mother's life is in danger; (C) Where there is a risk of suicide; (D) Where the pregnancy results from rape; (E) Where the pregnancy results from incest; (F) Where there is definitive evidence of physical or mental disability in the unborn child; (G) Should be available without restriction' [18 December]

	A	B	C	D	E	F	G
Total	22	44	17	34	28	11	12
Sex							
Male	19	47	20	33	27	11	12
Female	25	42	15	34	29	11	13
Age							
18–24	14	44	16	36	28	10	18
25–34	14	43	20	33	28	10	20
35–49	16	52	22	40	34	16	13
50–64	30	44	16	35	28	11	5
65+	42	34	10	18	18	6	3
Social Class							
ABC1	15	51	21	39	34	13	14
C2DE	25	41	17	32	26	12	13
F	30	42	10	25	21	5	5
Geographical							
Dublin	15	54	30	48	43	20	14
Rest of Leinster	24	42	14	29	25	12	11
Munster	24	37	9	26	18	6	12
Conn/Ulster	29	44	14	25	22	4	9
Urban/Rural							
Urban	19	46	19	36	31	14	15
Rural	27	41	14	30	24	7	8
Party							
FF	22	45	16	34	26	11	10
FG	26	47	18	36	34	14	5
Labour	17	47	22	33	29	12	19
PD	7	59	32	46	59	18	12
Green Party	11	63	28	54	50	22	3
Sinn Féin	18	44	17	31	22	10	23
Other	46	24	5	22	11	5	8
DK	21	42	15	29	27	7	18

Source: IMS.

Northern Ireland

TABLE 9.24

IRA

'Are you more or less tolerant now of the IRA following the terrorist attacks on the US, or is there no change in your attitude' [27 September]

	More Tolerant	Less Tolerant	Hasn't Changed
Total	7	29	58
Sex			
Male	8	24	64
Female	7	33	52
Age			
18–24	6	25	59
25–34	10	27	58
35–49	6	27	62
50–64	8	34	51
65+	5	32	58
Social Class			
ABC1	4	31	61
C2DE	10	26	56
F	5	35	56
Geographical			
Dublin	6	31	57
Rest of Leinster	12	26	53
Munster	5	26	61
Conn/Ulster	5	32	60
Urban/Rural			
Urban	7	29	60
Rural	7	29	55
Party			
FF	8	31	57
FG	3	37	56
Labour	8	33	54
PD	11	37	48
Green Party	6	23	66
Sinn Féin	24	14	59
Other	4	17	75
DK	4	20	63

Source: IMS.

TABLE 9.25

DECOMMISSIONING

	'Do you or do you not, believe the IRA should now begin the process of putting its weapons beyond use?' [27 September]	
	Should begin	Shouldn't begin
Total	85	8
Sex		
Male	84	10
Female	86	6
Age		
18–24	81	9
25–34	83	10
35–49	87	7
50–64	86	8
65+	85	7
Social Class		
ABC1	88	7
C2DE	80	10
F	93	3
Geographical		
Dublin	84	9
Rest of Leinster	81	7
Munster	87	7
Conn/Ulster	86	10
Urban/Rural		
Urban	83	9
Rural	87	7
Party		
FF	87	7
FG	91	6
Labour	84	10
PD	96	*
Green Party	80	17
Sinn Féin	55	33
Other	83	8
DK	80	5

Source: IMS.

European Union

TABLE 9.26

NICE TREATY REFERENDUM

'As you may know, three Referendums are being held on June 7th next on a number of issues. For each of the Referendums shown on this card, I would like you to tell me whether you are likely to vote Yes or No…(a) The Nice Treaty which provides, among other things, for the enlargement of the number of countries in the European Union'

Date of Poll[a]	Vote 1		Vote 2	
	Yes	No	Yes	No
Total	52	21	45	28
Sex				
Male	54	24	50	30
Female	50	18	40	26
Age				
18–24	56	17	42	28
25–34	49	21	48	21
35–49	55	20	44	29
50–64	49	25	47	33
65+	47	20	43	26
Social Class				
ABC1	59	20	47	26
C2DE	47	22	43	28
F	48	20	46	29
Geographical				
Dublin	48	24	49	27
Rest of Leinster	54	20	46	30
Munster	49	19	43	28
Conn/Ulster	59	20	40	25
Urban/Rural				
Urban	53	22	47	28
Rural	50	19	43	27
Party				
FF	57	17	51	23
FG	54	21	45	32
Labour	55	24	50	36
PD	69	17	65	25
Other	46	33	40	32
DK	36	18	32	27

[a]Vote 1: 14–15 May; Vote 2: 29–30 May.

Source: MRBI.

61

TABLE 9.27

IRELAND'S STATUS IN THE EU

'Which of the following statements comes closest to your view of Ireland's status within the EU: (1) Ireland should do all it can to unite fully with the EU; (2) Ireland should do all it can to protect its independence from the EU'.

Date of Poll[a]	Ireland/EU 1		Ireland/EU 2	
	1	2	1	2
Total	46	41	40	43
Sex				
Male	48	43	46	40
Female	45	39	34	45
Age				
18–24	47	37	48	35
25–34	50	38	39	42
35–49	52	39	43	40
50–64	38	46	36	48
65+	39	46	31	50
Social Class				
ABC1	55	37	46	39
C2DE	40	44	36	46
F	44	42	40	42
Geographical				
Dublin	43	44	40	42
Rest of Leinster	49	35	47	42
Munster	46	41	35	43
Conn/Ulster	47	43	37	44
Urban/Rural				
Urban	48	41	40	42
Rural	44	41	40	43
Party				
FF	51	38	41	43
FG	49	42	48	40
Labour	51	40	43	42
PD	55	45	60	35
Other	36	48	33	51
DK	37	39	31	40

[a]Ireland/EU 1: 14–15 May; Ireland/EU 2: 29–30 May.

Source: MRBI.

TABLE 9.28
NICE TREATY REFERENDUM 2002

'It is proposed to hold a new referendum on the Nice Treaty next year (2002). Will you vote in favour or against the Nice Treaty in the next referendum, or will you not vote at all?' [18 December]

	In Favour	Against	Not Vote
Total	30	27	14
Sex			
Male	35	29	12
Female	25	26	16
Age			
18–24	27	25	14
25–34	28	31	12
35–49	34	28	14
50–64	30	28	13
65+	28	23	18
Social Class			
ABC1	40	29	11
C2DE	25	26	15
F	24	27	14
Geographical			
Dublin	31	28	12
Rest of Leinster	38	27	10
Munster	24	26	17
Conn/Ulster	25	28	17
Urban/Rural			
Urban	31	28	14
Rural	27	26	13
Party			
FF	35	25	13
FG	33	28	11
Labour	36	30	14
PD	38	23	6
Green Party	26	42	10
Sinn Féin	25	41	10
Other	8	58	6
DK	19	22	15

Source: IMS.

TABLE 9.29

EU AND STATE AID

'Finally, in the aftermath of the terrorist attacks in the US, Aer Lingus has been forced to cut back its operations by 25 per cent, with a possible 1,600 jobs at risk. The EU, however, bans all state aid to airlines, preventing national governments from offering financial support. In the present circumstances should this EU ban remain or should it be suspended to enable state payments to airlines such as Air Lingus?' [27 September]

	Remain	Suspended
Total	25	57
Sex		
Male	28	56
Female	22	58
Age		
18–24	21	56
25–34	24	59
35–49	26	59
50–64	33	51
65+	20	61
Social Class		
ABC1	24	62
C2DE	26	53
F	23	59
Geographical		
Dublin	26	58
Rest of Leinster	20	56
Munster	28	56
Conn/Ulster	28	58
Urban/Rural		
Urban	27	58
Rural	24	56
Party		
FF	24	60
FG	24	61
Labour	26	61
PD	19	63
Green Party	43	54
Sinn Féin	37	59
Other	29	54
DK	27	44

Source: IMS.

TABLE 9.30

NICE TREATY ISSUES

'How well do you feel you understand the issues involved in the Nice Treaty? 1) Have a good understanding of what the Treaty is about; 2) Understand some of the issues but not all; 3) Am only vaguely aware of the issues involved; 4) Do not know what the Treaty is about at all'

Date of Poll[a]	Issues 1				Issues 2			
	1	2	3	4	1	2	3	4
Total	11	26	32	30	15	32	31	19
Sex								
Male	15	30	29	25	21	34	28	15
Female	6	22	34	36	10	30	34	24
Age								
18–24	7	22	32	37	9	30	33	23
25–34	7	30	32	31	17	25	31	26
35–49	12	29	30	27	16	34	34	15
50–64	11	26	31	30	17	35	31	16
65+	15	18	34	29	17	35	27	18
Social Class								
ABC1	14	29	31	24	18	34	30	16
C2DE	8	23	31	36	13	30	33	22
F	8	27	36	26	18	34	29	17
Geographical								
Dublin	9	25	27	36	13	33	30	23
Rest of Leinster	10	28	35	24	18	38	29	15
Munster	11	26	36	26	16	28	35	17
Conn/Ulster	12	24	27	36	15	29	31	22
Urban/Rural								
Urban	12	29	29	28	16	33	30	20
Rural	9	21	35	34	14	31	34	18
Party								
FF	12	27	28	31	14	35	32	17
FG	13	26	38	22	16	38	29	16
Labour	7	31	29	33	21	25	38	14
PD	7	38	28	24	15	40	45	*
Other	12	25	28	32	17	32	32	16
DK	6	17	37	36	14	22	28	33

[a]Issue 1: 14–15 May; and Issue 2: 29–30 May.

Source: MRBI.

TABLE 9.31

ENLARGEMENT

	'The European Union proposes to admit up to 13 new member-states over the next 10 years. Are you in favour or against the enlargement of the EU in this way?' [14–15 May]	
	Favour	Against
Total	59	23
Sex		
Male	60	28
Female	57	22
Age		
18–24	59	19
25–34	62	23
35–49	58	27
50–64	54	31
65+	58	24
Social Class		
ABC1	70	21
C2DE	52	27
F	50	31
Geographical		
Dublin	58	27
Rest of Leinster	59	23
Munster	56	26
Conn/Ulster	62	25
Urban/Rural		
Urban	61	27
Rural	55	24
Party		
FF	65	21
FG	57	29
Labour	61	29
PD	59	38
Other	51	28
DK	49	26

Source: MRBI.

TABLE 9.32

COMMISSION MEMBERSHIP

'When the number of member-states reaches 27, the right of each state to have a Commissioner will rotate so that there will be limited periods when Ireland (and each other country in turn) will have no Commissioner' Acceptable/ Unacceptable [29–30 May]

	Acceptable	Unacceptable
Total	34	46
Sex		
Male	40	45
Female	29	47
Age		
18–24	30	48
25–34	35	44
35–49	35	48
50–64	37	47
65+	31	41
Social Class		
ABC1	36	49
C2DE	34	43
F	32	50
Geographical		
Dublin	36	44
Rest of Leinster	38	50
Munster	28	47
Conn/Ulster	36	41
Urban/Rural		
Urban	34	47
Rural	35	45
Party		
FF	34	48
FG	42	42
Labour	36	49
PD	60	35
Other	28	56
DK	28	36

Source: MRBI.

TABLE 9.33

COUNCIL OF MINISTERS

Ireland's share of the votes in the EU Council of Ministers will be reduced from 3.45% of the votes in a Union of 15 members to 2.02% in a Union of 27 members' Acceptable/Unacceptable [29–30 May]

	Acceptable	Unacceptable
Total	38	40
Sex		
Male	46	37
Female	30	43
Age		
18–24	34	41
25–34	41	37
35–49	39	44
50–64	39	41
65+	34	38
Social Class		
ABC1	42	43
C2DE	36	38
F	34	45
Geographical		
Dublin	40	38
Rest of Leinster	43	44
Munster	32	42
Conn/Ulster	35	37
Urban/Rural		
Urban	38	41
Rural	38	40
Party		
FF	38	44
FG	48	37
Labour	32	51
PD	70	25
Other	38	40
DK	27	33

Source: MRBI.

TABLE 9.34

RAPID REACTION FORCE 1

	Participate	Opt Out
'The EU has established the military Rapid Reaction Force for peacekeeping and peace enforcement in the European area. Do you think that 1) Ireland should participate in the Rapid Reaction Force or 2) Ireland should negotiate to opt out from participation in the Rapid Reaction Force?' [14–15 May]		
Total	50	29
Sex		
Male	57	30
Female	45	27
Age		
18–24	50	27
25–34	46	32
35–49	53	28
50–64	54	26
65+	47	29
Social Class		
ABC1	53	29
C2DE	49	28
F	47	26
Geographical		
Dublin	47	35
Rest of Leinster	50	24
Munster	60	19
Conn/Ulster	43	39
Urban/Rural		
Urban	51	30
Rural	49	27
Party		
FF	52	28
FG	54	23
Labour	47	28
PD	69	21
Other	48	38
DK	42	28

Source: MRBI.

TABLE 9.35

RAPID REACTION FORCE 2

'The EU has established the military Rapid Reaction Force for humanitarian tasks, peacekeeping and peace making. Do you think that 1) Ireland should participate in the Rapid Reaction Force or 2) Ireland should negotiate to opt out from participation in the Rapid Reaction Force?'[29–30 May]

	Participate	Opt Out
Total	49	32
Sex		
Male	54	32
Female	43	32
Age		
18–24	52	27
25–34	47	33
35–49	51	33
50–64	47	35
65+	44	30
Social Class		
ABC1	51	33
C2DE	48	31
F	42	31
Geographical		
Dublin	58	29
Rest of Leinster	50	36
Munster	43	30
Conn/Ulster	40	35
Urban/Rural		
Urban	52	32
Rural	44	32
Party		
FF	52	29
FG	49	35
Labour	51	37
PD	70	25
Other	47	35
DK	39	32

Source: MRBI.

Neutrality

TABLE 9.36

NEUTRALITY

	Neutrality: 'Do you think Ireland should continue or discontinue its policy of military neutrality?' [14–15 May]	
	Continue	Discontinue
Total	72	16
Sex		
Male	69	21
Female	74	11
Age		
18–24	72	14
25–34	74	15
35–49	73	17
50–64	68	16
65+	69	18
Social Class		
ABC1	70	19
C2DE	72	15
F	77	10
Geographical		
Dublin	70	19
Rest of Leinster	68	15
Munster	74	15
Conn/Ulster	74	15
Urban/Rural		
Urban	71	17
Rural	72	14
Party		
FF	73	17
FG	71	16
Labour	78	14
PD	72	17
Green Party	–	–
Sinn Féin	–	–
Other	70	19
DK	67	12

Source: MRBI.

TABLE 9.37

IRISH AIRPORTS AND THE USAF

'The Irish Government has offered the US landing and refuelling facilities at Irish airports in the war against international terrorism. Which of the following best describes your own opinion: Allowing the US to land and refuel at Irish airports is the appropriate level of support for Ireland to offer; Ireland should support the US in a more significant way by participating in military action with the US and its allies; or Ireland should not offer any level of support at all to the US?' [27 September]

	Appropriate	More	None
Total	63	9	18
Sex			
Male	69	10	15
Female	58	9	20
Age			
18–24	63	12	16
25–34	63	8	20
35–49	64	9	18
50–64	67	9	15
65+	58	10	19
Social Class			
ABC1	66	9	16
C2DE	61	10	19
F	66	8	15
Geographical			
Dublin	65	11	16
Rest of Leinster	62	9	18
Munster	65	9	15
Conn/Ulster	61	8	23
Urban/Rural			
Urban	64	12	15
Rural	62	6	21
Party			
FF	67	10	14
FG	63	12	16
Labour	59	5	26
PD	59	19	15
Green Party	74	3	14
Sinn Féin	53	14	22
Other	50	17	29
DK	61	6	21

Source: IMS.

Referendums on the Death Penalty and International Criminal Court

TABLE 9.38

REFERENDUM ON DEATH PENALTY

'As you may know, three Referendums are being held on June 7th next on a number of issues. For each of the Referendums shown on this card, I would like you to tell me whether you are likely to vote Yes or No...(b) The removal from the Constitution of any provision for the death penalty'

Date of Poll[a]	Death 1		Death 2	
	Yes	No	Yes	No
Total	55	28	51	31
Sex				
Male	57	29	50	36
Female	53	26	51	26
Age				
18–24	55	23	52	31
25–34	58	28	53	27
35–49	57	29	49	33
50–64	51	31	48	34
65+	51	26	50	29
Social Class				
ABC1	62	26	58	26
C2DE	50	28	44	35
F	52	31	54	28
Geographical				
Dublin	53	26	51	27
Rest of Leinster	48	33	57	38
Munster	59	25	51	33
Conn/Ulster	60	28	47	26
Urban/Rural				
Urban	54	28	54	30
Rural	57	27	45	33
Party				
FF	57	26	55	31
FG	60	31	51	33
Labour	59	28	53	33
PD	45	34	60	40
Other	60	26	50	31
DK	41	27	39	28

[a]Dates of opinion poll fieldwork: Death 1 and ICC 1: 14–15 May; and Death 2 and ICC 2: 29–30 May.

TABLE 9.39

REFERENDUM ON INTERNATIONAL CRIMINAL COURT

As you may know, three Referendums are being held on June 7th next on a number of issues. For each of the Referendums shown on this card, I would like you to tell me whether you are likely to vote Yes or No... (c) A provision enabling Ireland to allow an international criminal court to try cases of genocide, crimes against humanity and war crimes'

Date of Poll[a]	ICC 1		ICC 2	
	Yes	No	Yes	No
Total	65	11	64	13
Sex				
Male	70	12	70	13
Female	60	11	57	12
Age				
18–24	63	10	59	11
25–34	70	13	65	11
35–49	71	9	70	12
50–64	60	13	62	16
65+	56	13	57	14
Social Class				
ABC1	73	11	70	11
C2DE	61	13	61	14
F	59	6	58	10
Geographical				
Dublin	62	13	66	12
Rest of Leinster	67	8	73	11
Munster	66	12	62	12
Conn/Ulster	65	12	50	17
Urban/Rural				
Urban	66	12	67	12
Rural	63	10	59	14
Party				
FF	67	12	67	13
FG	72	10	67	12
Labour	62	15	74	11
PD	79	*	85	5
Other	64	14	60	21
DK	54	9	49	8

[a]Dates of opinion poll fieldwork: Death 1 and ICC 1: 14–15 May; and Death 2 and ICC 2: 29–30 May.

Tribunals

TABLE 9.40

TRIBUNALS

'The failure to co-operate with the Tribunals of Inquiry has resulted in Liam Lawlor TD, receiving a three month jail sentence from the courts. Do you think the Tribunals in the operation of their investigations have: too little power, too much power or just the right amount of power?' [1 February]

	Too Little Power	Too Much Power	Just Right Amount
Total	39	13	39
Sex			
Male	41	15	39
Female	38	12	40
Age			
18–24	36	13	40
25–34	41	12	38
35–49	42	14	39
50–64	42	9	39
65+	30	21	38
Social Class			
ABC1	43	11	40
C2DE	39	14	37
F	30	16	43
Geographical			
Dublin	50	12	32
Rest of Leinster	37	11	44
Munster	33	14	43
Conn/Ulster	34	18	39
Urban/Rural			
Urban	44	13	36
Rural	32	14	44
Party			
FF	36	15	42
FG	41	10	43
Labour	41	15	36
PD	27	21	52
Green Party	60	5	28
Sinn Féin	43	16	32
Other	30	14	48
DK	42	15	31

Source: IMS.

TABLE 9.41

LAWLOR AND FLOOD TRIBUNAL

Lawlor 1: 'Are you or are you not satisfied with the way the Flood Tribunal and the courts have dealt with Liam Lawlor TD?'; Lawlor 2: 'Are you or are you not satisfied with the way the Government has responded to the Liam Lawlor case?'; Lawlor 3: 'In your opinion, should Mr Lawlor now resign from the Dail or not?' [22–23 January]

	Lawlor 1		Lawlor 2		Lawlor 3	
	Satisfied	Not Satisfied	Satisfied	Not Satisfied	Resign	Not Resign
Total	64	25	34	53	85	7
Sex						
Male	64	29	34	58	86	8
Female	63	22	34	47	83	6
Age						
18–24	56	28	34	46	83	7
25–34	62	28	33	51	85	8
35–49	66	23	31	58	87	5
50–64	69	24	33	59	84	8
65 +	62	24	43	42	82	8
Social Class						
ABC1	72	21	35	57	86	8
C2DE	57	28	33	49	83	7
F	64	26	35	53	85	5
Geographical						
Dublin	64	25	25	60	86	6
Rest of Leinster	63	26	39	50	83	7
Munster	64	26	30	57	87	7
Conn/Ulster	65	23	48	36	83	9
Urban/Rural						
Urban	62	27	31	58	87	6
Rural	65	22	39	45	81	9
Party						
FF	64	24	47	40	83	9
FG	70	21	30	59	89	6
Labour	66	28	22	75	94	4
PD	78	22	34	63	97	3
Other	56	34	26	58	84	4
DK	60	24	24	55	78	7

Source: MRBI.

Government Formation

TABLE 9.42

COALITION PREFERENCE

'Most observers believe that the outcome of the next General Election will lead to the formation of another Coalition Government. If this were to happen, which one of these Coalition options would you prefer?' [29–30 May]

	FF/PD/Ind	FF/Lab	FG/Lab	FG/Lab/PD	FG/Lab/GP
Total	38	13	15	6	11
Sex					
Male	38	14	17	6	10
Female	38	12	14	6	12
Age					
18–24	38	13	12	3	13
25–34	36	11	14	4	12
35–49	38	15	13	6	12
50–64	36	15	17	8	10
65+	43	9	22	8	8
Social Class					
ABC1	36	14	14	7	15
C2DE	37	14	15	5	9
F	49	6	20	10	9
Geographical					
Dublin	29	16	11	5	14
Rest of Leinster	39	11	17	5	13
Munster	38	15	15	9	9
Conn/Ulster	50	7	20	4	8
Urban/Rural					
Urban	32	15	13	6	14
Rural	46	10	19	6	8
Party					
FF	67	20	4	1	1
FG	7	2	49	16	22
Labour	4	25	36	3	26
PD	65	*	*	25	5
Other	27	7	8	3	23
DK	25	10	5	8	7

Source: MRBI.

TABLE 9.43

SINN FÉIN IN GOVERNMENT

	'Would you or would you not accept Sinn Féin as part of the next Coalition Government?' [29–30 May]	
	Yes	No
Total	47	41
Sex		
Male	54	39
Female	41	42
Age		
18–24	55	27
25–34	49	37
35–49	48	39
50–64	40	51
65+	44	49
Social Class		
ABC1	48	41
C2DE	50	37
F	33	54
Geographical		
Dublin	51	41
Rest of Leinster	44	44
Munster	41	43
Conn/Ulster	56	32
Urban/Rural		
Urban	50	40
Rural	44	42
Party		
FF	49	40
FG	33	57
Labour	53	37
PD	50	45
Other	64	28
DK	42	36

Source: MRBI.

TABLE 9.44

COALITION ALTERNATIVES

'If the results of the next General Election fail to allow the existing Government Coalition of Fianna Fail and the PD's (Progressive Democrats) to form a Government, which, if any, of these alternatives would you prefer?' [18 December]

	FF/PD/Ind	FF/Lab	FG/Lab	FG/Lab/PD	FG/Lab/GP
Total	27	10	14	20	9
Sex					
Male	25	14	15	21	9
Female	28	6	13	20	9
Age					
18–24	19	10	10	14	12
25–34	28	12	14	14	10
35–49	25	13	14	23	10
50–64	28	8	16	24	8
65+	33	5	17	27	4
Social Class					
ABC1	30	11	14	20	8
C2DE	24	10	16	19	9
F	28	12	9	28	10
Geographical					
Dublin	25	12	16	18	10
Rest of Leinster	29	12	14	22	4
Munster	24	6	15	23	11
Conn/Ulster	30	12	10	20	10
Urban/Rural					
Urban	25	11	16	18	10
Rural	28	9	11	25	8
Party					
FF	44	13	19	5	6
FG	5	2	4	70	10
Labour	8	2	30	42	8
PD	69	9	4	3	13
Green Party	7	6	25	19	26
Sinn Féin	9	54	3	8	17
Other	37	8	8	25	11
DK	13	7	9	11	9

Source: IMS.

TABLE 9.45

SINN FÉIN IN GOVERNMENT

| | 'If the next general election in the Republic results in a hung Dáil, where Sinn Féin holds the balance of power, do you think that Sinn Féin Ministers should be included in any Coalition government, even if there is no evidence of IRA decommissioning?' [27 September] | |
	Yes	No
Total	37	45
Sex		
Male	44	43
Female	30	48
Age		
18–24	43	33
25–34	44	40
35–49	34	49
50–64	33	56
65+	31	47
Social Class		
ABC1	34	52
C2DE	39	39
F	35	51
Geographical		
Dublin	35	51
Rest of Leinster	36	40
Munster	32	49
Conn/Ulster	49	38
Urban/Rural		
Urban	39	45
Rural	34	45
Party		
FF	37	46
FG	23	63
Labour	47	41
PD	26	70
Green Party	43	51
Sinn Féin	100	*
Other	38	54
DK	28	34

Source: IMS.

80

Electoral Participation

TABLE 9.46

INTEREST

'In overall terms, can you tell me the extent to which you are interested in current affairs – the political social, economic affairs of the country?' Response Options: 1) Very Uninterested; 2) Fairly Uninterested; 3) Neither Interested nor Uninterested; 4) Fairly Interested; 5) Very Interested. [22–23 January]

	1	2	3	4	5
Total	4	11	13	45	27
Sex					
Male	3	6	11	48	32
Female	5	17	15	42	22
Age					
18–24	9	17	18	44	11
25–34	4	12	13	47	23
35–49	3	12	11	46	28
50–64	1	7	11	38	42
65+	2	9	16	47	27
Social Class					
ABC1	1	7	9	46	38
C2DE	6	15	16	42	21
F	3	9	15	51	21
Geographical					
Dublin	5	10	12	43	30
Rest of Leinster	3	10	13	48	26
Munster	3	10	15	46	25
Conn/Ulster	2	18	11	41	28
Urban/Rural					
Urban	4	13	13	43	27
Rural	3	10	13	47	27
Party					
FF	3	9	12	49	27
FG	3	9	14	40	33
Labour	*	12	14	49	25
PD	*	3	3	41	53
Other	2	13	12	43	31
DK	9	18	19	39	16

Source: MRBI.

81

TABLE 9.47

PARTICIPATION

	'For yourself, do you always vote, vote most times, vote some of the time, seldom vote or never vote?' Response Options: 1) Always Vote; 2) Vote Most Times; 3) Vote Some Times; 4) Seldom Vote; 5) Never Vote. [22–23 January]				
	1	2	3	4	5
Total	69	17	6	5	4
Sex					
Male	71	14	7	4	4
Female	66	19	5	5	4
Age					
18–24	38	16	13	13	19
25–34	63	20	7	7	2
35–49	69	19	5	5	1
50–64	84	12	3	*	*
65+	85	12	3	1	*
Social Class					
ABC1	79	14	3	3	2
C2DE	62	18	8	6	5
F	66	18	7	6	3
Geographical					
Dublin	69	13	7	7	4
Rest of Leinster	65	19	6	5	5
Munster	72	15	7	4	2
Conn/Ulster	68	23	3	3	3
Urban/Rural					
Urban	70	14	6	5	4
Rural	67	20	6	4	3
Party					
FF	75	17	3	2	2
FG	81	10	3	5	1
Labour	66	18	9	6	2
PD	66	19	9	6	*
Other	62	20	8	5	6
DK	53	16	11	10	10

Source: MRBI.

Funding Political Parties

TABLE 9.48

CORPORATE DONATIONS

'Political opinion is divided on the role of corporate donations in the funding of political parties. Some say corporate donations should be banned altogether, others argue these should be retained. Which are you in favour of – retaining corporate donations or imposing an outright ban' [8 March]

	In Favour	Against
Total	22	61
Sex		
Male	21	63
Female	24	60
Age		
18–24	26	56
25–34	17	64
35–49	20	60
50–64	29	58
65+	22	53
Social Class		
ABC1	26	59
C2DE	20	63
F	–	–
Geographical		
Dublin	23	64
Rest of Leinster	26	55
Munster	19	61
Conn/Ulster	23	57
Urban/Rural		
Urban[a]	23	64
Rural[b]	22	58
Party		
FF	31	51
FG	22	76
Labour	13	69
PD	25	58
Green Party	10	80
Sinn Féin	14	74
Other	5	79
DK	21	58

[a]Urban refers to Dublin; [b]rural refers to areas other than Dublin.

Source: IMS.

TABLE 9.49
STATE FUNDING OF POLITICAL PARTIES

	If corporate donations were banned would you accept that any short fall in the funding of political parties should be financed through taxation or not? [8 March]	
	Yes	No
Total	17	71
Sex		
Male	24	67
Female	11	75
Age		
18–24	13	74
25–34	13	77
35–49	24	65
50–64	15	73
65+	17	68
Social Class		
ABC1	19	72
C2DE	15	71
F	–	–
Geographical		
Dublin	19	71
Rest of Leinster	13	65
Munster	10	81
Conn/Ulster	36	57
Urban/Rural		
Urban[a]	19	71
Rural[b]	15	72
Party		
FF	19	72
FG	25	73
Labour	24	68
PD	8	92
Green Party	10	85
Sinn Féin	16	77
Other	21	63
DK	9	68

[a]Urban refers to Dublin; [b]rural refers to areas other than Dublin.

Source: IMS.

Opinion Poll Details (Number of Respondents)

TABLE 9.50

OPINION POLL DETAILS, 2001

Organisation For	MRBI IT	MRBI IT	MRBI IT	IMS SI	IMS SI*	IMS SI	IMS SI	IMS** II
Date	22–3 Jan.	14–15 May	29–30 May	1 Feb.	8 March	17 May	27 Sept.	18 Dec.
Total	1000	1000	1000	1109	646	1104	1100	1068
Sex								
Male	492	490	494	545	305	534	538	523
Female	508	510	506	564	341	570	562	545
Age								
18–24	144	158	165	200	133	203	194	176
25–34	230	210	205	223	147	216	219	224
35–49	284	286	282	313	177	319	317	281
50–64	203	182	203	222	117	215	217	224
65+	139	164	145	151	72	151	153	163
Social Class								
ABC1	370	377	368	365	289	384	380	352
C2DE	499	499	507	583	357	567	570	556
F	131	124	125	161	–	153	150	160
Geographical								
Dublin	288	290	290	333	337	333	310	320
Rest of Leinster	252	240	250	257	110	261	253	256
Munster	292	289	281	320	155	311	330	299
Conn/Ulster	168	181	179	199	44	199	207	192
Urban/Rural								
Urbanª	590	581	582	644	337	633	630	651
Ruralᵇ	410	419	418	465	309	471	470	417
Party								
FF	379	391	398	409	239	433	449	457
FG	151	178	183	219	63	209	196	160
Labour	102	85	76	101	68	111	92	92
PD	32	28	20	33	12	24	27	32
Green Party	–	–	–	40	20	43	35	31
Sinn Féin	–	–	–	37	43	34	49	44
Other	160	138	149	44	19	22	24	35
DK	176	179	174	145	118	164	169	154

IT = Irish Times, SI = Sunday Independent, II = Irish Independent.

*Urban areas only; **weighted; ªfor 8 March poll: urban refers to Dublin; ᵇfor 8 March poll: rural refers to areas other than Dublin.

NORTHERN IRELAND

Compiled by Ian O'Flynn
School of Politics, Queen's University Belfast

1. Government Ministers

TABLE 1.1

NORTHERN IRELAND OFFICE (31 DECEMBER 2001)

Secretary of State	Dr John Reed
Minister of State	Jane Kennedy
Parliamentary Under Secretary of State	Des Brown
Conservative Opposition Spokesperson	Quentin Davies

TABLE 1.2

NORTHERN IRELAND EXECUTIVE (31 DECEMBER 2001)

Office of the First Minister and Deputy First Minister	
First Minister	David Trimble (UUP)
Deputy First Minister	Mark Durkan (SDLP)
Junior Minister	Denis Haughy (SDLP)
Junior Minister	Dermot Nesbitt (UUP)
Assembly Ministers	
Department of Enterprise, Trade and Investment	Sir Reg Empey (UUP)
Department of Finance and Personnel	Sean Farren (SDLP)
Department for Regional Development	Peter Robinson (DUP)
Department of Education	Martin McGuinness (SF)
Department of Culture, Arts and Leisure	Michael McGimpsey (UUP)
Department of Higher and Further Education	Sean Farren (SDLP)
Department for Employment and Training	Carmel Hannah (SDLP)
Department for Social Development	Maurice Morrow (DUP)
Department of Health, Social Services and Public Safety	Bairbre de Brún (SF)
Department of the Environment	Sam Foster (UUP)
Department of Agriculture and Rural Development	Brid Rodgers (SDLP)

2. State of the Parties

TABLE 2.1

UNITED KINGDOM HOUSE OF COMMONS

Party	31 December 2000	31 December 2001
Ulster Unionist Party	9	6
Democratic Unionist Party	3	5
Social Democratic and Labour Party	3	3
Sinn Féin	2	4
United Kingdom Unionist Party	1	–
Total	18	18

TABLE 2.2

NORTHERN IRELAND ASSEMBLY (NO. OF SEATS)

Party	31 December 2000	31 December 2001
Ulster Unionist Party	28	26
Social Democratic and Labour Party	24	24
Democratic Unionist Party*	20	21
Sinn Féin	18	18
Alliance	6	6
United Kingdom Unionist Party	1	1
Progressive Unionist Party	2	2
Northern Ireland Women's Coalition	2	2
Northern Ireland Unionist Party	3	3
United Unionist Assembly Party	3	3
Independent Unionist**	1	2
Total	108	108

* Former Independent Unionist Roger Hutchinson joined the DUP on 19 January 2001;
** Includes Peter Weir (ceased to be a member of UUP) and Pauline Armitage (suspended from UUP) from 9 November 2001.

3. Parliamentary Committees

TABLE 3.1

NORTHERN IRELAND MPS ON HOUSE OF COMMONS SELECT COMMITTEES
(31 DECEMBER 2001)

Regulatory Reform	Jeffrey Donaldson (UUP)
Statutory Instruments	Jeffrey Donaldson (UUP)
Transport Committee	Gregory Campbell (DUP)
Transport, Local Government and the Regions	Gregory Campbell (DUP)

TABLE 3.2

NORTHERN IRELAND AFFAIRS SELECT COMMITTEE (31 DECEMBER 2001)

Michael Mates (Con) Chairman
Adrian Bailey (Lab)
Harry Barnes (Lab)
Roy Beggs (UUP)
Henry Bellingham (Con)
Tony Clarke (Lab)
Stephen McCabe (Lab)
Eddie McGrady (SDLP)
Stephen Pound (Lab)
Peter Robinson (DUP)
Rev. Martin Smyth (UUP)
Mark Tami (Lab)
Bill Tynan (Lab)

TABLE 3.3

NORTHERN IRELAND: COMMITTEES OF THE NORTHERN IRELAND
ASSEMBLY (31 DECEMBER 2001)

Comittee	Chair	Deputy Chair
Departmental Committees		
Agriculture and Rural Development Statutory Committee	Ian Paisley (DUP)	George Savage (UUP)
Culture, Arts and Leisure Committee	Eamon O'Neill (SDLP)	Mick Murphy (SF)
Education Committee	Danny Kennedy (UUP)	Sammy Wilson (DUP)
Employment and Learning Committee	Esmond Birnie (UUP)	Mervyn Carrick (DUP)
Enterprise, Trade and Investment Committee	Pat Doherty (SF)	Sean Neeson (All)
Environment Committee	William McCrea (DUP)	Patricia Lewsley SDLP)
Finance and Personnel Committee	Francie Molloy (SF)	Roy Beggs (UUP)
Health, Social Services and Public Safety Statutory Committee	Joe Hendron (SDLP)	Tommy Gallagher (SDLP)
Regional Development Statutory Committee	Alban Maginness (SDLP)	Alan McFarland (UUP)
Social Development Statutory Committee	Fred Cobain (UUP)	Gerry Kelly (SF)
Standing Committees		
Procedures Committee	Pat McNamee (SF)	Duncan Shipley-Dalton (UUP)
Business Committee	Lord Alderdice of Knock (All)	Denis Watson (UUAP)
Committee of the Centre	Edwin Poots (DUP)	Oliver Gibson (DUP)
Public Accounts Committee	William Bell (UUP)	Conor Murphy (SF)
Committee on Standards and Privileges	Donovan McClelland (SDLP)	Derek Hussey (UUP)
Audit Committee	John Dallat (SDLP)	Billy Hutchinson (PUP)
Ad-Hoc Committees		
Ad Hoc Committee on Flags (NI) Order 2000 (reported to the Assembly 10/10/2000)	Fraser Agnew (UUAP)	David Ford (All)
Ad Hoc Committee – Financial Investigations (NI) Order 2000 (reported to the Assembly 6/02/2001)	Billy Bell (UUP)	Alban Maginnnes (SDLP)
Ad Hoc Committee – Life Sentences (NI) Order 2000 (reported to the Assembly 12/03/2001)	George Savage (UUP)	Eileen Bell (All)
Ad Hoc Committee – Proceeds of Crime Bill (reported to the Assembly 29/05/2001)	Alban Maginness (SDLP)	John Gorman (UUP)
Ad Hoc Committee on Criminal Injuries Compensation (reported to the Assembly 15/11/2001)	Roger Hutchinson (DUP)	Kieran McCarthy (All)
Ad Hoc Committee on Disqualification Legislation	Duncan Shipley Dalton (UUP)	Eileen Bell (All)

4. Bills Enacted

Acts of the Northern Ireland Assembly

1. *Dogs (Amendment) Act (NI) 2001*. Makes provision for the destruction of dogs under the Dogs (Northern Ireland) Order 1983. [29 January 2001]
2. *Planning (Compensation, etc.) Act (NI) 2001*. Abolishes the right to compensation in respect of certain planning decisions. [20 March 2001]
3. *Health and Personal Social Services Act (NI) 2001*. Establishes a Northern Ireland Social Care Council and make provision for the registration, regulation and training of social care workers; makes provision about the recovery of charges in connection with the treatment of road traffic casualties in health services hospitals; amends the law about the health and personal social services; to confer power to regulate the profession of pharmaceutical chemist; and for connected purposes. [20 March 2001]
4. *Fisheries (Amendment) Act (NI) 2001*. Amends the Fisheries Act (Northern Ireland) 1966 with regard to regulation of sea-fisheries in Northern Ireland inshore waters. [20 March 2001]
5. *Ground Rents Act (NI) 2001*. Makes provision for the redemption of certain ground rents and other periodic payments. [20 March 2001]
6. *Government Resources and Accounts Act (NI) 2001*. Makes provisions with regard to government resources and accounts as well as for connected purposes (with special reference to consolidated fund). [22 March 2001]
7. *Budget Act (NI) 2001*. Authorises the issue out of the Consolidated Fund of certain sums for the service of the years ending 31st March 2001 and 2002; appropriates those sums for specified purposes and amends certain appropriations in aid for the year ending 31st March 2001; authorises the Department of Finance and Personnel to borrow on the credit of the appropriated sums; and authorises the use for the public service of certain resources for the year ending 31st March 2002. [22 March 2001]
8. *Street Trading Act (NI) 2001*. Provides for the licensing of street traders; designation of streets; offences and enforcement of penalties. [5 April 2001]
9. *Electronic Communications Act (NI) 2001*. Makes provision to facilitate the use of electronic communications and electronic data storage, including powers to modify legislation. [5 April 2001]
10. *Defective Premises (Landlord's Liability) Act (NI) 2001*. Amends the law as to the liability of landlords for injury or damage caused to persons through defects in the state of premises let under certain tenancies. Also covers Landlord's duty of care by virtue of obligation to repair premises demised. [2 July 2001]
11. *Adoption (Intercounty Aspects) Act (NI) 2001*. Makes provision for giving effect to the Convention on Protection of Children and Co-operation in respect of Intercountry Adoption concluded at the Hague on 29th May 1993; makes further provision in relation to adoptions with an international element; and for connected purposes. [2 July 2001]
12. *Familty Law Act (NI) 2001*. Makes further provision for the acquisition of parental responsibility under Article 7 of the Children (Northern Ireland) Order 1995; and provides for certain presumptions of parentage and for tests to determine parentage. [17 July 2001]
13. *Product Liability (Amendment) Act (NI) 2001*. Amends Part II of the Consumer Protection (Northern Ireland) Order 1987. [20 July 2001]
14. *Trustee Act (NI) 2001*. Amends the law relating to trustees and persons having the investment powers of trustees; deals with the duty of care; issues of investment; acquisition of land, and questions of renumeration. [20 July 2001]
15. *Department for Employment and Learning Act (NI) 2001*. Renames the Department of Higher and Further Education, Training and Employment as the Department for Employment and Learning
16. *Budget (No.2) Act (NI) 2001*. Authorises the issue out of the Consolidated Fund of certain sums for the service of the year ending 31st March 2002; appropriates those

sums for specified purposes; authorises the Department of Finance and Personnel to borrow on the credit of the appropriated sums; authorises the use for the public service of certain resources (including accruing resources) for the year ending 31st March 2002; and repeals certain spent enactments. [20 July 2001]

17. *Social Security Fraud Act (NI) 2001.* Makes provision, for the purposes of the law relating to social security, about the obtaining and disclosure of information; makes provision for restricting the payment of social security benefits in the case of persons convicted of offences relating to such benefits and about the institution of proceedings for such offences; and for connected purposes. [15 November 2001]

Acts of the UK Parliament (Public Acts) 2001

1. *Criminal Justice and Police Act 2001.* Makes provision for combatting crime and disorder; makes provisions for the disclosure of information relating to criminal matters and about powers of search and seizure; amends the Police and Criminal Evidence Act 1984, the Police and Criminal Evidence (Northern Ireland) Order 1989 and the Terrorism Act 2000; makes provision about the police, the National Criminal Intelligence Service and the National Crime Squad; makes provision about the powers of the courts in relation to criminal matters; and for connected purposes. [11 May 2001]

2. *Anti-Terrorism, Crime and Security Act 2001.* Reforms previous counter-terrorist legislation, including extension of police powers of identifications in Northern Ireland. [14 December 2001]

Orders in Council 2001

1. *The Financial Investigations (NI) Order 2001.* This Order amends Part IV of the Proceeds of Crime (Northern Ireland) Order 1996 (NI 9). Covers investigations into the extent or whereabouts of property held or transferred within the previous 6 years; provides a power to require a solicitor to provide information as to whether a specified person was a client of his in respect of certain matters and about the nature of any transaction relating to them; and other related issues. [14 May 2001]

2. *The Police (NI) Order 2001.* This Order amends two provisions of the Police (Northern Ireland) Act 2000. Section 41, which deals with trainees, is amended so that, before the Northern Ireland Policing Board is established, references to the Board are to be construed as references to the Police Authority for Northern Ireland. Section 76 is amended so that draft orders under sections 47(3) (renewal of temporary provisions on recruitment) and 54 (emblems and flags) are subject to the affirmative resolution procedure rather than the procedure provided for in section 6 of the Statutory Instruments Act 1946. [18 July 2001]

3. *The Life Sentences (NI) Order 2001.* This Order provides for the release and recall of persons serving a sentence of life imprisonment or detention during the pleasure of the Secretary of State. Relates to Commissioners' procedure; tariffs; release on license; licenses and recall.

5. Main Political Events of 2001

January

14 **Policing:** SDLP leader John Hume hits out at Secretary of State Peter Mandelson for suggesting that his party's refusal to endorse planned policing reforms was driven by electoral considerations.

15 **United Nations:** High Commissioner for Human Rights Mary Robinson says that the murder of solicitor Rosemary Nelson is a matter of 'widespread concern' at the highest levels of the United Nations.

19 **Secretary of State:** High Court hears that Sinn Féin wants Secretary of State Peter Mandelson to be cross-examined in a bid to block the Union flag being flown above buildings used by its ministers.

25 **Resignation:** A row over applications for British citizenship forces Peter Mandelson to step down as Secretary of State for Northern Ireland. Dr John Reed appointed as his replacement.

30 **Good Friday Agreement (GFA):** First Minister David Trimble's ban on Sinn Féin ministers attending North/South meetings declared unlawful by a high court judge in Belfast.

February

16 **GFA:** As impasse over policing, decommissioning and demilitarisation continues, UUP leader David Trimble signals that his party may move for a formal review of the Agreement.

23 **Policing:** The Catholic Bishop of Derry Dr Seamus Hegarty calls for respect for any person's decision to join the PSNI.

March

2 **Decommissioning:** Proposed North/South Ministerial Council meeting postponed as First Minister David Trimble and three other UUP members of the Northern Ireland Executive refuse to attend in protest at the IRA's lack of progress on decommissioning.

4 **Decommissioning:** The Catholic Primate of Ireland Archbishop Sean Brady calls for progress on decommissioning.

8 **Decommissioning:** IRA issues statement indicating its intention to enter into further discussions with General John de Chastelain's decommissioning body.

9 **Decommissioning:** Following mixed reaction among the North's political parties, Northern Secretary Dr John Reid claims that substantive moves by the IRA on decommissioning were required before the British government could act on policing and demilitarisation.

April

4 **Policing:** Nationalist and republican politicians criticise publicity surrounding interest in the planned new Police Service of Northern Ireland, claiming it will take 25 years to achieve 50/50 cross-community recruitment.

9 **Reconciliation Fund:** Irish Foreign Affairs minister Brian Cowen pledges IR£372,625 from his department's Reconciliation Fund will be allocated to 45 organisations in Northern Ireland involved in a wide range of cross-community, educational, research and outreach activities.

12 **GFA:** Dissident Irish republican splinter group, the Real IRA, vows to step up its terrorist campaign, fuelling fears that hardliners will use the ongoing impasse in the peace process to launch a wave of attacks in Northern Ireland and England.

27 **Equality Legislation:** Northern Ireland Civil Service announces proposals for ambitious equality legislation, including implementing a Single Equality Bill in 2002 which would bring together all existing anti-discrimination legislation.

30 **Bloody Sunday:** The disclosure that Martin McGuinness was second-in-command of the IRA in Derry on Bloody Sunday provokes DUP calls for the removal from office of the Sinn Féin education minister.

May

8   **Decommissioning:** UUP leader David Trimble claims he will resign as First Minister within eight weeks if the IRA does not begin to disarm by 1 July. The move was seen in the North as a high-risk effort to avoid heavy UUP losses in the forthcoming general election.

18   **Election:** The SDLP launches its election campaign with a confident message that the Good Friday agreement is working and the people will not allow it to be destroyed.

21   **Election:** At the launch of his party's election manifesto, UUP leader David Trimble insists his resignation ultimatum will stand if there is no movement on arms decommissioning by the IRA.

30   **Decommissioning:** It is confirmed that the IRA has opened up two of its secret arms dumps for further examination and has had another meeting with the head of the independent decommissioning body General John de Chastelain.

June

7   **Election:** Polling takes place across Northern Ireland for both the local government and general elections. It is the first time that both elections have been held on the same day, with 100 candidates contesting 18 parliamentary seats and 982 candidates running for 582 local council seats. Significant election gains for Sinn Féin and DUP at the expense of SDLP and UUP. David Trimble under pressure to bow to hardliners within his party.

20   **Decommissioning:** In a hardline statement, IRA says that it will not bow to unionist or British government pressure on arms decommissioning.

23   **Decommissioning:** Intensive negotiations under way to try to prevent UUP leader David Trimble resigning his post as First Minister on 1 July as decommissioning deadlock continues.

July

1   **Resignation:** UUP leader David Trimble resigns as First Minister, automatically triggering the removal of SDLP Deputy First Minister Seamus Mallon. By law, the British Government must call fresh elections to the Northern Ireland Assembly or suspend it by 12 August.

2   **Parade:** Contentious Orange Order Drumcree parade banned amid the continuing political crisis and deadlock over paramilitary decommissioning.

10   **GFA:** UFF confirms that its ceasefire remains in place but withdraws its support for the Agreement.

12   **Parade:** Orange Order parades end in violence and rioting.

14   **Weston Park:** Weston Park Peace talks aimed at rescuing the Good Friday Agreement: The British and Irish governments announce their intention to draft a set of proposals which they will present to the political parties on the outstanding issues.

18   **GFA:** During Prime Minister's Question Time at Westminster, Tony Blair pledges that the package being prepared by the British and Irish governments for presentation to the Northern Ireland parties will be fair and reasonable.

August

1   **GFA:** Pro-Agreement parties receive non-negotiable proposals which the British and Irish governments believe should lead to full implementation of the Good Friday Agreement. Areas addressed include decommissioning, policing and security normalisation, along with a draft all-party statement on its institutions.

6 **Decommissioning:** The IRA proposes a method for putting guns completely and verifiably beyond use. UUP leader David Trimble states that the IRA has taken a significant step but indicated that it falls short of actually beginning decommissioning.

7 **GFA:** The SDLP welcomes the proposals which emerged from the Weston Park negotiations, and claims that proposals for a new police service were now closer to the Patten Commission's original recommendations.

10 **Suspension:** Northern Ireland Assembly temporarily suspended. One-day break in devolution allows the parties at the Assembly six more weeks to elect a First and Deputy First Minister.

13 **Colombia:** Credibility of IRA cease-fire comes under renewed doubts as three suspected IRA members are arrested in Colombia charged with training FARC guerrillas.

14 **Decommissioning:** In response to the suspension of devolution, the IRA withdraw its proposal for decommissioning, deepening the political crisis in Northern Ireland.

17 **Policing:** The revised police implementation plan is published, replacing a version of the document unveiled last year. Republican and unionist hardliners signal their opposition to aspects of the plan.

20 **Policing:** The SDLP announces its decision to endorse the new arrangements for policing in Northern Ireland.

27 **Policing:** UUP member Jeffrey Donaldson calls for unionist unity to exclude Sinn Féin from the assembly and stop the progress of the revised implementation plan on policing.

September

1 **Holy Cross:** The pupils of Holy Cross Catholic Girls Primary School, who are aged between four and 11, run loyalist gauntlet on the first day of the new term.

10 **GFA:** Assembly members sit for the first full meeting of the autumn session. Less than two weeks remain, however, before the Northern Secretary Dr John Reid must decide again whether to suspend the Assembly or else call elections if it fails to elect a new First and Deputy First Minister.

11 **Colombia:** Cuba's foreign minister claims that one of the three suspected IRA members arrested in Colombia had been Sinn Féin's representative in his country for a number of years. Sinn Féin president Gerry Adams denies this claim.

17 **SDLP:** John Hume today announces that he is to step down as leader of the SDLP.

20 **SDLP:** Séamus Mallon, who was the favourite to succeed John Hume as leader of the SDLP, rules himself out of the contest.

20 **Policing:** The SDLP announces that its three nominations to the new Policing Board are Eddie McGrady MP, and assembly members Joe Byrne and Alex Attwood.

22 **Suspension:** Secretary of State for Northern Ireland John Reid suspends devolution for a further one-day period, a technicality which gives the Belfast Assembly six more weeks of life. The move was made in the hope that progress would be achieved in arms decommissioning by early November. The tactic was opposed by the UUP and Sinn Féin.

28 **SDLP:** Mark Durkan to become new leader of SDLP.

October

1 **DUP:** A DUP sponsored motion, attempting to exclude Sinn Féin from the Northern Ireland Executive, has gathered the required 30 signatures for an assembly debate.

7 **GFA:** Sinn Féin MP Michelle Gildernew warns that unionist threats to expel republicans from the Northern Ireland Assembly would not advance demands for IRA decommissioning.

8 **UUP:** Northern Ireland's political institutions are thrown into crisis as UUP threaten a phased withdrawal of ministers from the power-sharing executive.

20 **Colombia:** Sinn Féin leader Gerry Adams admits that one of three Irishmen captured in Colombia was the party's representative in Cuba.

21 **Decommissioning:** In an unprecedented step, Sinn Féin President Gerry Adams calls for the IRA to move on the arms issue. Decommissioning expected to begin within days.

25 **Decommissioning:** A clear sequence of political events unfolds following the IRA's arms move, with three UUP ministers back in the executive along with a rolling programme of demolishing security installations. DUP ministers Peter Robinson and Nigel Dodds also returning to the Assembly.

27 **UUP:** UUP Executive backs David Trimble's nomination for re-election as First Minister of the Northern Ireland Assembly.

29 **First Minister:** In order to boost UUP leader David Trimble's chances as re-election as First Minister in the face of anti-Agreement unionist opposition, the Women's Coalition floats the possibility of temporarily redesignating as 'unionist.'

November

3 **First Minister:** In order to ensure that a majority of unionists, as well as a majority of nationalists, support the re-election of UUP party leader David Trimble as First Minister, Alliance party Assembly members redesignate as 'unionist.'

5 **Policing:** Police Service of Northern Ireland formally comes into being, replacing Royal Ulster Constabulary.

6 **First Minister:** Despite legal action by DUP on redesignation, UUP party leader David Trimble re-elected as First Minister with SDLP party leader-elect Mark Durkan elected as Deputy First Minister.

8 **Policing:** Sinn Féin once again rules out endorsing the new policing arrangements – on the same day as the inaugural meeting of the new Policing Board.

11 **SDLP:** Mark Durkan formally takes over as leader of SDLP with Brid Rodgers winning a tight contest for deputy leader.

18 **GAA:** Rule 21, the GAA's controversial ban on police and members of the British Army playing football and hurling, abolished at a special congress in Dublin.

December

3 **Election:** DUP deputy leader Peter Robinson seeks a judicial review of the election of Northern Ireland's First and Deputy First Ministers. If successful, the election for the next assembly could be brought forward from 1 May 2003, the date fixed by the secretary of state John Reid.

14 **Executive:** SDLP MLA Sean Farren is named finance minister in the Stormont Executive as part of SDLP leader Mark Durkan's reshuffle of ministerial portfolios.

16 **Leaders Meet:** Sinn Féin president Gerry Adams leaves Belfast for a three-day trip to South America which will include a meeting with the Cuban leader Fidel Castro.

6. Election Results

TABLE 6.1

WESTMINSTER ELECTIONS (NI) THURSDAY 7 JUNE 2001

Party	Seats	Vote (%)
Ulster Unionist Party	6	26.76
Democratic Unionist Party	5	22.46
Sinn Féin	4	21.71
Social Democratic and Labour Party	3	20.96
Alliance Party of Northern Ireland	0	3.58
United Kingdom Unionist Party	0	1.67
Independent Ulster Unionist	0	0.84
Progressive Unionist Party	0	0.59
Northern Ireland Women's Coalition	0	0.37
Conservative Party	0	0.30
Workers' Party	0	0.29
Northern Ireland Unionist Party	0	0.22
Other Candidates	0	0.26

TABLE 6.2

NORTHERN IRELAND CONSTITUENCY RESULTS (ELECTED CANDIDATE)

Constituency	Candidate	Party	Votes	% share
East Antrim	Roy Beggs	UUP	13,101	36.29
North Antrim	Ian Paisley	DUP	24,539	49.86
South Antrim	David Burnside	UUP	16,366	37.06
Belfast East	Peter Robinson	DUP	15,667	42.53
Belfast North	Nigel Dodds	DUP	16,718	40.84
Belfast South	Martin Symth	UUP	17,008	44.81
Belfast West	Gerry Adams	SF	27,096	66.12
North Down	Sylvia Hermon	UUP	20,833	56.02
South Down	Eddie McGrady	SDLP	24,136	46.35
Fermanagh and South Tyrone	Michelle Gildernew	SF	17,739	34.13
Foyle	John Hume	SDLP	24,538	50.20
Lagan Valley	Jeffrey Donaldson	UUP	25,966	56.52
East Londonderry	Gregory Campbell	DUP	12,813	32.14
Mid Ulster	Martin McGuinness	SF	25,502	51.07
Newry and Armagh	Seamus Mallon	SDLP	20,784	37.37
Strangford	Iris Robinson	DUP	18,532	42.84
West Tyrone	Pat Doherty	SF	19,814	40.83
Upper Bann	David Trimble	UUP	17,095	33.50

TABLE 6.3

LOCAL GOVERNMENT ELECTIONS (NI) THURSDAY 7 JUNE 2001

Party	First Preference Votes	Vote (%)	Seats
Ulster Unionist Party	181,336	23	154
Democratic Unionist Party	169,477	21	131
Sinn Féin	163,269	21	108
Social Democratic and Labour Party	153,424	19	117
Alliance Party of Northern Ireland	40,443	5	28
Others	82,119	11	44
Total	790,068	100	582

TABLE 6.4

DISTRIBUTION OF SEATS ON THE 26 DISTRICT COUNCILS

District Council	UUP	DUP	SDLP	SF	APNI	Others	No. of Seats
Antrim	7	5	5	2	0	0	19
Ards	8	9	1	0	4	1	23
Armagh	7	4	6	5	0	0	22
Ballymena	7	11	4	0	0	2	24
Ballymoney	5	8	2	1	0	0	16
Banbridge	7	5	3	0	1	1	17
Belfast	11	10	9	14	3	4	51
Carrickfergus	4	6	0	0	5	2	17
Castlereagh	5	10	2	0	4	2	23
Coleraine	10	7	4	0	0	1	22
Cookstown	3	2	4	6	0	1	16
Craigavon	8	6	7	4	0	1	26
Derry	2	4	14	10	0	0	30
Down	6	2	10	4	0	1	23
Dungannon	6	3	4	8	0	1	22
Fermanagh	7	2	4	9	0	1	23
Larne	4	5	2	0	2	2	15
Limavady	3	2	4	4	0	2	15
Lisburn	13	5	3	4	3	2	30
Magherafelt	2	3	3	7	0	1	16
Moyle	3	3	4	1	0	4	15
Newry and Mourne	4	1	10	13	0	2	30
Newtownabbey	9	8	2	1	1	4	25
North Down	8	5	0	0	5	7	25
Omagh	3	2	6	8	0	2	21
Strabane	2	3	4	7	0	0	16

7. Opinion Polls

All figures are percentages.

Party Support

TABLE 7.1

PARTY SUPPORT

	Which Northern Ireland political party would you support?									
	UUP	SDLP	DUP	All.	SF	PUP	UDP	WC	Other	Don't know
Total	19	20	10	3	9	1	1	1	1	15
Sex										
Male	22	21	9	3	10	1	1	0	1	11
Female	18	20	10	3	7	0	1	1	0	18
Age										
18–24	11	12	9	1	9	1	2	1	0	30
25–34	12	16	12	4	10	1	1	2	1	15
35–44	15	18	10	1	11	0	0	2	1	18
45–54	19	27	8	3	9	1	1	0	1	10
55–65	24	24	13	3	10	1	1	1	0	10
65+	31	21	8	5	3	0	1	1	1	12
Religion										
Catholic	1	47	1	2	20	0	0	1	1	14
Protestant	37	1	19	4	0	1	2	1	0	14
No religion	8	10	6	5	6	1	0	3	1	21

Source: 'Life and Times' survey <http://www.ark.ac.uk/nilt.html>.

TABLE 7.2

ELECTORAL PARTICIPATION

	Talking to people about the general election on the 7th of June, we have found that a lot of people didn't manage to vote. How about you – did you manage to vote in the general election?	
	Yes, voted	No
Total	66	34
Sex		
Male	69	31
Female	64	36
Age		
18–24	35	65
25–34	57	43
35–44	67	33
45–54	69	31
55–65	79	21
65+	74	26
Religion		
Catholic	73	27
Protestant	69	31
No religion	33	67

Source: 'Life and Times' survey <http://www.ark.ac.uk/nilt.html>.

TABLE 7.3

PARTY VOTE

	If response to voted is 'yes,' which party did you vote for in the general election?									
	UUP	SDLP	DUP	All.	SF	PUP	UDP	WC	Other	Don't know
Total	26	27	14	2	12	1	1	1	1	5
Sex										
Male	29	26	13	2	14	2	2	0	1	4
Female	23	28	15	3	10	1	1	1	1	6
Age										
18–24	20	21	16	4	21	3	2	2	0	7
25–34	20	25	21	2	15	2	2	2	1	3
35–44	18	25	16	2	16	1	1	1	2	10
45–54	23	35	11	3	12	1	1	0	0	3
55–65	29	30	15	2	11	0	2	0	0	3
65+	40	24	10	3	4	0	1	1	2	5
Religion										
Catholic	2	57	0	2	25	0	0	1	1	4
Protestant	47	2	27	3	0	2	2	1	1	5
No religion	*	*	*	*	*	*	*	*	*	*

Source: 'Life and Times' survey <http://www.ark.ac.uk/nilt.html>.

National Identity

TABLE 7.4
NATIONAL QUESTION

National Question: Generally speaking, do you think of yourself as a unionist, a nationalist or neither?

	Unionist	Nationalist	Neither	Other	Don't know
Total	35	27	35	1	2
Sex					
Male	40	21	28	*	1
Female	32	24	40	1	2
Age					
18–24	26	24	48	*	1
25–34	31	23	43	*	3
35–44	30	33	36	*	1
45–54	30	30	37	1	2
55–65	42	31	24	2	2
65+	51	20	28	1	1
Religion					
Catholic	*	65	33	1	2
Protestant	70	*	28	1	1
No religion	17	9	71	*	3

Source: 'Life and Times' survey <http://www.ark.ac.uk/nilt.html>.

TABLE 7.5
NATIONALITY

Nationality: Please say which, if any, of the following describes the way you think of yourself. Please choose as many or as few as apply.

	British	English	Euro.	Irish	North Irish	Scots	Ulster	Other	None of these
Total	45	2	4	30	27	1	9	1	3
Sex									
Male	45	2	5	33	27	1	11	1	2
Female	45	2	3	28	28	1	8	1	3
Age									
18–24	34	1	1	35	33	1	9	1	4
25–34	46	3	6	27	36	1	10	2	2
35–44	42	2	5	35	28	1	8	1	2
45–54	44	1	5	30	23	1	8	1	2
55–65	49	1	2	31	22	1	9	1	2
65+	52	1	2	21	25	1	12	1	4
Religion									
Catholic	12	1	4	65	28	*	1	1	2
Protestant	73	2	2	4	27	2	16	1	2
No religion	45	6	11	16	35	1	6	4	8

Source: 'Life and Times' survey <http://www.ark.ac.uk/nilt.html>.

Future of Northern Ireland

TABLE 7.6

FUTURE OF NORTHERN IRELAND

Do you think the long-term policy for Northern Ireland should be for it to remain part of the UK, to reunify with the rest of Ireland, or to become an independent state?

	Remain part of the UK	Reunify with the rest of Ireland	Become an independent state	Other opinions
Total	50	28	6	2
Sex				
Male	49	32	6	3
Female	50	24	6	2
Age				
18–24	49	26	8	2
25–34	49	24	10	2
35–44	45	30	8	1
45–54	45	32	6	2
55–65	54	30	4	3
65+	54	30	4	3
Religion				
Catholic	15	59	6	3
Protestant	79	5	5	2
No religion	46	16	10	5

Source: 'Life and Times' survey <http://www.ark.ac.uk/nilt.html>.

TABLE 7.7

ACCEPT UNITED IRELAND?

If the majority of people in Northern Ireland ever voted to become part of a United Ireland do you think you would find this: A) almost impossible to accept; B) would not like it, but could live with it; C) would happily accept the wishes of the majority?

	A	B	C
Total	18	36	39
Sex			
Male	19	40	36
Female	17	33	41
Age			
18–24	19	31	39
25–34	16	39	36
35–44	18	36	39
45–54	20	31	41
55–65	20	38	37
65+	15	39	40
Religion			
Catholic	2	16	72
Protestant	26	44	26
No religion	6	26	53

Source: 'Life and Times' survey <http://www.ark.ac.uk/nilt.html>.

TABLE 7.8

FUTURE OF NORTHERN IRELAND

Which of these statements comes closest to your view?
(A) Northern Ireland should become independent: separate from UK and European Union; (B) Northern Ireland should become independent: separate from UK, but part of European Union; (C) Northern Ireland should remain part of the UK, with its own elected parliament which has law-making & taxation powers; (D) Northern Ireland should remain part of the UK with its own elected assembly which has limited law-making powers only; (E) Northern Ireland should remain part of the UK without an elected assembly; (F) Northern Ireland should unify with the Republic of Ireland.

	A	B	C	D	E	F
Total	3	7	31	12	13	21
Sex						
Male	4	6	32	12	11	25
Female	2	8	30	12	13	19
Age						
18–24	5	9	33	5	9	19
25–34	3	8	31	12	10	18
35–44	3	9	28	10	16	25
45–54	3	10	29	14	13	24
55–65	2	4	28	15	17	24
65+	3	5	38	13	11	15
Religion						
Catholic	4	9	14	4	7	49
Protestant	2	6	47	18	17	1
No religion	2	9	26	13	13	8

Source: 'Life and Times' survey <http://www.ark.ac.uk/nilt.html>.

TABLE 7.9

POSSIBILITY OF UNITED IRELAND

At any time in the next 20 years, do you think it is likely or unlikely that there will be a United Ireland?

	Very likely	Quite likely	Quite unlikely	Very unlikely	Even chance
Total	14	29	18	20	6
Sex					
Male	15	29	19	22	6
Female	13	29	17	19	6
Age					
18–24	6	32	18	24	9
25–34	11	26	24	21	5
35–44	16	32	15	19	5
45–54	20	26	15	17	6
55–65	12	27	19	25	5
65+	12	31	17	17	6
Religion					
Catholic	15	29	18	19	6
Protestant	13	31	18	21	6
No religion	11	21	13	20	10

Source: 'Life and Times' survey <http://www.ark.ac.uk/nilt.html>.

Attitudes towards the Assembly

TABLE 7.10

ASSEMBLY

Which of the following do you think has most influence over the way Northern Ireland is run?

	NI Assembly	UK Government	NI Local Councils	EU	Other
Total	28	51	7	4	2
Sex					
Male	28	53	6	6	2
Female	28	49	7	3	2
Age					
18–24	21	55	8	2	1
25–34	30	50	6	4	3
35–44	32	47	8	4	1
45–54	28	55	7	3	3
55–65	27	51	6	4	4
65+	28	49	7	7	1
Religion					
Catholic	27	53	8	5	1
Protestant	29	50	6	4	3
No religion	25	50	7	5	2

Source: 'Life and Times' survey <http://www.ark.ac.uk/nilt.html>.

TABLE 7.11

ASSEMBLY VOICE

From what you have heard so far, do you think that having a Northern Ireland Assembly is giving Northern Ireland a stronger voice in the United Kingdom; a weaker voice in the United Kingdom; it is making no difference?

	Stronger	Weaker	No Difference
Total	42	11	38
Sex			
Male	43	10	42
Female	42	13	35
Age			
18–24	35	11	40
25–34	39	14	38
35–44	40	12	39
45–54	46	12	37
55–65	46	9	39
65+	46	10	34
Religion			
Catholic	55	5	32
Protestant	33	16	43
No religion	40	13	34

Source: 'Life and Times' survey <http://www.ark.ac.uk/nilt.html>.

TABLE 7.12

ASSEMBLY GOVERNANCE

From what you have seen and heard so far, do you think that having a Northern Ireland Assembly is giving ordinary people more say in how Northern Ireland is governed; less say; it is making no difference?

	More	Less	No Difference
Total	40	8	44
Sex			
Male	44	6	45
Female	36	9	44
Age			
18–24	28	7	54
25–34	38	8	46
35–44	37	8	45
45–54	44	9	42
55–65	43	8	45
65+	43	7	41
Religion			
Catholic	51	3	39
Protestant	41	12	50
No religion	37	8	40

Source: 'Life and Times' survey <http://www.ark.ac.uk/nilt.html>.

TABLE 7.13

MLAS SOLVE PROBLEMS

How much would you say that members of the Northern Ireland Assembly from different parties work together to help solve Northern Ireland's problems?

	Great deal	Fair amount	Not very much	Not at all
Total	6	37	35	15
Sex				
Male	6	39	36	15
Female	6	37	34	16
Age				
18–24	3	30	32	21
25–34	5	34	39	16
35–44	6	37	38	15
45–54	5	42	34	16
55–65	10	37	33	16
65+	8	41	33	12
Religion				
Catholic	8	47	32	8
Protestant	6	33	36	8
No religion	2	24	41	21

Source: 'Life and Times' survey <http://www.ark.ac.uk/nilt.html>.

TABLE 7.14

WILL ASSEMBLY REMAIN?

	Do you think that the Assembly will still be in place in three years time?	
	Yes	No
Total	15	14
Sex		
Male	60	16
Female	56	13
Age		
18–24	51	19
25–34	54	17
35–44	61	14
45–54	64	12
55–65	60	13
65+	53	12
Religion		
Catholic	69	8
Protestant	52	19
No religion	45	15

Source: 'Life and Times' survey <http://www.ark.ac.uk/nilt.html>.

Attitudes to the Good Friday Agreement

TABLE 7.15

THE GOOD FRIDAY AGREEMENT

	Thinking back to the Good Friday Agreement, now, would you say that: (A) unionists benefited a lot more than nationalists; (B) unionists benefited a little more than nationalists; (C) nationalists benefited a lot more than unionists; (D) nationalists benefited a little more than unionists; (E) unionists and nationalists benefited equally; (F) other; (G) neither side benefited.						
	A	B	C	D	E	F	G
Total	2	2	31	11	31	1	14
Sex							
Male	2	1	33	12	33	1	13
Female	1	2	29	10	30	1	14
Age							
18–24	3	4	27	12	19	1	17
25–34	2	0	28	12	30	1	14
35–44	2	2	30	11	33	0	13
45–54	1	2	31	9	30	0	19
55–65	0	0	28	11	41	1	12
65+	1	1	37	10	30	1	10
Religion							
Catholic	3	2	10	10	47	1	18
Protestant	1	1	52	11	19	0	9
No religion	0	4	14	10	29	0	23

Source: 'Life and Times' survey <http://www.ark.ac.uk/nilt.html>.

TABLE 7.16

GOOD FRIDAY AGREEMENT VOTE TODAY

	If the vote on the Good Friday Agreement was held again today, how would you vote?			
	Yes	No	Wouldn't vote	Don't know
Total	50	20	14	10
Sex				
Male	51	23	14	8
Female	50	18	14	12
Age				
18–24	41	14	14	22
25–34	48	20	18	9
35–44	48	24	16	8
45–54	52	20	14	9
55–65	54	22	11	7
65+	53	18	9	12
Religion				
Catholic	75	3	11	7
Protestant	34	36	13	11
No religion	34	14	26	18

Source: 'Life and Times' survey <http://www.ark.ac.uk/nilt.html>.

TABLE 7.17

GOOD FRIDAY VOTE 1998

	How did you vote in 1998 when a referendum on the Agreement was held?			
	Yes	No	Didn't vote	Don't know
Total	55	14	15	5
Sex				
Male	57	16	16	3
Female	54	12	15	7
Age				
18–24	22	10	21	4
25–34	49	14	23	5
35–44	55	16	16	7
45–54	62	14	13	3
55–65	66	15	9	3
65+	63	13	10	7
Religion				
Catholic	71	3	14	5
Protestant	48	24	13	5
No religion	37	7	31	7

Source: 'Life and Times' survey <http://www.ark.ac.uk/nilt.html>.

Attitudes to Policing and Decommissioning

TABLE 7.18

POLICING

There has been a lot of debate in recent years about policing in Northern Ireland. Thinking about the fairness of the police, do you think that the police treat: (A) Catholics much better than Protestants; (B)Catholics a bit better than Protestants; (C) Both equally; (D) Protestants a bit better than Catholics; (E) Protestants much better than Catholics.

	A	B	C	D	E
Total	4	4	63	10	7
Sex					
Male	4	3	63	9	6
Female	4	4	63	9	6
Age					
18–24	5	5	54	9	13
25–34	4	5	61	12	7
35–44	4	3	58	15	9
45–54	3	3	70	7	7
55–65	4	4	65	11	6
65+	2	4	69	8	5
Religion					
Catholic	0	1	55	19	16
Protestant	7	6	71	4	0
No religion	4	4	60	7	5

Source: 'Life and Times' survey <http://www.ark.ac.uk/nilt.html>.

TABLE 7.19

RELATIVE IN POLICE

Suppose a close relative of yours was thinking about becoming a police officer here in Northern Ireland. Would you encourage them to join, discourage them from joining, or neither?

	Encourage	Discourage	Neither	It depends
Total	40	23	25	7
Sex				
Male	42	25	25	6
Female	38	22	26	8
Age				
18–24	36	17	29	10
25–34	38	27	23	5
35–44	34	32	24	6
45–54	41	21	25	9
55–65	39	23	26	8
65+	48	15	28	5
Religion				
Catholic	32	29	29	6
Protestant	47	19	23	6
No religion	37	20	24	13

Source: 'Life and Times' survey <http://www.ark.ac.uk/nilt.html>.

TABLE 7.20

POLICING REFORM

| | Do you think that the reform of the police in Northern Ireland has gone too far, has not gone far enough, or is it about right? | | |
	Gone too far	Not gone far enough	About right
Total	31	21	33
Sex			
Male	34	24	31
Female	29	18	34
Age			
18–24	29	22	27
25–34	30	18	37
35–44	28	28	32
45–54	29	24	33
55–65	34	21	33
65+	38	13	35
Religion			
Catholic	3	44	38
Protestant	59	4	27
No religion	19	13	41

Source: 'Life and Times' survey <http://www.ark.ac.uk/nilt.html>.

TABLE 7.21

ARMY BASES

| | Is shutting army bases important for peace? | | | | |
	Agree strongly	Agree	Neither strongly	Disagree	Disagree
Total	10	28	18	24	14
Sex					
Male	10	30	17	26	14
Female	10	27	19	22	15
Age					
18–24	11	26	17	25	13
25–34	9	27	18	25	14
35–44	15	26	17	23	14
45–54	11	25	22	27	11
55–65	9	36	16	19	18
65+	5	28	19	26	17
Religion					
Catholic	21	47	15	11	2
Protestant	2	13	19	34	27
No religion	7	27	21	26	8

Source: 'Life and Times' survey <http://www.ark.ac.uk/nilt.html>.

TABLE 7.22

REPUBLICAN DECOMMISSIONING

	Should there be an assembly before republican decommissioning?				
	Agree strongly	Agree	Neither agree nor disagree	Disagree	Disagree strongly
Total	25	23	11	26	9
Sex					
Male	24	21	12	29	11
Female	26	24	11	24	7
Age					
18–24	27	24	14	22	4
25–34	22	23	14	26	8
35–44	22	25	9	24	14
45–54	23	26	11	28	7
55-65	28	17	11	32	9
65+	31	22	10	25	6
Religion					
Catholic	8	16	12	41	18
Protestant	40	28	10	16	2
No religion	21	24	14	22	8

Source: 'Life and Times' survey <http://www.ark.ac.uk/nilt.html>.

TABLE 7.23

LOYALIST DECOMISSIONING

	Should there be an assembly before loyalist decommissioning?				
	Agree strongly	Agree	Neither agree nor disagree	Disagree	Disagree strongly
Total	23	25	12	26	8
Sex					
Male	21	24	13	29	10
Female	24	26	12	24	6
Age					
18–24	19	30	17	21	5
25–34	20	25	14	26	8
35–44	20	27	10	26	11
45–54	22	27	11	27	7
55–65	25	19	12	33	7
65+	28	23	11	25	6
Religion					
Catholic	10	18	12	39	15
Protestant	34	29	12	18	2
No religion	20	27	14	20	7

Source: 'Life and Times' survey <http://www.ark.ac.uk/nilt.html>.